FOLKLORE & WITCHCRAFT
OF
THE CORNISH VILLAGE

Edited by Kelvin I. Jones

OAKMAGIC PUBLICATIONS

FOLKLORE & WITCHCRAFT
OF THE CORNISH VILLAGE

Edited by Kelvin I Jones

Published by OAKMAGIC PUBLICATIONS
2004

ISBN: 1 904330 52 5

Pps: 47 - 57: C. K.I. Jones
Pps: 78 - 9: C. K.I. Jones

Pps: 1 - 34: From "Choice Notes", published
C. 1880 as part of "Notes & Queries". (T.Q. Couch
and other contributors.)

Pps: 35 - 39: First published in "The Cornish Review",
C. William Paynter, 1922.

Pps: 58 - 63: First published as part of the Transactions
of the Penzance Natural History & Antiquarian Society,
1888.

Pps: 4 - 77: First published in "Old Cornwall".(Various volumes)
Also: pps. 40 - 46. C. Wm. Paynter.

Pps 30 31: From "Old Cornwall."

OAKMAGIC PUBLICATIONS,
P.O. BOX 67,
MONMOUTH NP25 3YP.

For a catalogue of over 100 British folklore titles,
send SAE to the publishers at this address.

www.oakmagicpublications.com

THE FOLK LORE OF A CORNISH VILLAGE.

Having pleasingly occupied my leisure in getting together all that is noteworthy respecting the past history and present condition of the place of my birth, I have thought that those chapters which treat of its folk lore might find an appropriate place in " N. & Q.," if abridged, and modified to suit its pages. Though the papers in another shape were read some time since before a provincial antiquarian society, they have never been published.

The place, whose popular antiquities are here to be recorded, is situated on the eminently romantic coast of the south-eastern part of Cornwall. The bold bluff hills resting by the sea-line on a margin of craggy transition slate, alike attractive to the artist and interesting to the geologist, have here, seemingly, suffered some disruption, and in the fissure is dropped the village, its houses resting on ledges in the hills, or skirting the inlets of the sea which forms its harbour. The inland country, for some distance, is a rapid succession of well-cultivated hill and " coomb," for that can

1

scarcely be called *valley* which is but the acute junction of the bases of opposite hills. The population is part seafaring, part agricultural, and in reference to education as well off as such people generally are. In this quiet corner lurk many remnants of faded creeds, and ancient usages which have vanished from districts more subject to mutation with the circumstances which gave rise to them, as the side eddies of a stream retain those sticks and straws which the current would have swept off to the ocean. I begin with an account of our fairy mythology.

Though the piskies, in spite of the prognostications of the poets, have outlived the " grete charite and prayers " of the limitour, and the changes in politics and religion which took place " when Elizabeth and later James came in," it is scarcely to be expected that they will withstand that great exorcist, *steam*, when it shall make its appearance among us, and there is the greater need that " all the fairies' evidence " should be entrusted to your safe keeping.

The belief in the little folk is far from dead, though the people of the present generation hold it by a slighter tenure than their forefathers did, and are aware that piskies are *now* fair objects of ridicule, whatever they formerly were. One old woman in particular, to whose recital of some of the following tales I have listened in mute attention, was a firm believer in them; and I remember her pettish reply, when a young friend of mine ventured to hint a doubt: " What! not believe in 'em, when my poor mother had been pinched black and blue by 'em." The argument was conclusive, for we could not then see its fallacy, though we have since learnt that the poor soul in question had not the kindest of husbands.

This creed has received so many additions and modifications at one time, and has suffered so many abstractions at another, that it is impossible to make any arrangement of our fairies into classes.

" The elves of hills, brooks, standing lakes, and groves "

are all now confounded under the generic name *pisky*.

F 4

Some of the later interpolations are of a very obvious character, as will hereafter be pointed out. Our piskies are little beings standing midway between the purely spiritual, and the material, suffering a few at least of the ills incident to humanity. They have the power of making themselves seen, heard, and felt. They interest themselves in man's affairs, now doing him a good turn, and anon taking offence at a trifle, and leading him into all manner of mischief. The rude gratitude of the husbandman is construed into an insult, and the capricious sprites mislead him on the first opportunity, and laugh heartily at his misadventures. They are great enemies of sluttery, and great encouragers of good husbandry. When not singing and dancing, their chief nightly amusement is in riding the colts, and plaiting their manes, or tangling them with the seed-vessels of the burdock. Of a particular field in this neighbourhood it is reported that the farmer never puts his horses in it but he finds them in the morning in a state of great terror, panting, and covered with foam. Their form of government is monarchical, as frequent mention is made of the "king of the piskies." We have a few stories of pisky changelings, the only proof of whose parentage was, that "they didn't goodey" (thrive). It would seem that fairy children of some growth are occasionally entrusted to human care for a time, and recalled; and that mortals are now and then kidnapped, and carried off to fairy land; such, according to the nursery rhyme, was the end of Margery Daw :—

> "See-saw, Margery Daw
> Sold her bed, and lay upon straw;
> She sold her straw, and lay upon hay,
> Piskies came and carri'd her away."

A disposition to laughter is a striking trait in their character. I have been able to gather little about the personalities of these creatures. My old friend before mentioned used to describe them as about the height of a span, clad in green, and having straw hats, or little red caps on their heads. Two only are known by name, and I have heard them addressed in the following rhyme : —

3

"Jack o' the lantern! Joan the wad!
Who tickled the maid and made her mad,
Light me home, the weather's bad."

I leave the stories of the *piskys-led*, of which this neighbourhood can furnish several *authentic* instances, for the following ancient legends, all careful copies of oral traditions.

Colman Grey.—A farmer, who formerly lived on an estate in our vicinity, was returning one evening from a distant part of the farm, when, in crossing a particular field, he saw, to his surprise, sitting on a stone in the middle of it, a miserable-looking little creature, human in appearance, though diminutive in size, and apparently starving with cold and hunger. Pitying its condition, and perhaps aware that it was of elfish origin, and that good luck would amply repay him for his kind treatment of it, he took it home, placed it by the warm hearth on a stool, and fed it with nice milk. The poor bantling soon recovered from the lumpish and only half-sensible state in which it was found, and, though it never spoke, became very lively and playful. From the amusement which its strange tricks excited, it became a general favourite in the family, and the good folk really felt very sorry when their strange guest quitted them, which he did in a very unceremonious manner. After the lapse of three or four days, as the little fellow was gamboling about the farm kitchen, a shrill voice from the *town-place* or farmyard, was heard to call three times, " Colman Grey ! " at which he sprang up, and gaining voice, cried " Ho ! ho ! ho ! my daddy is come," flew through the key-hole, and was never afterwards heard of.

A Voyage with the Piskies. — About a mile to the eastward of us is a pretty bay, on the shores of which may be seen the picturesque church of Talland, the hamlet of Portallow, with its scattered farm-houses, and the green on which the children assemble at their sports. In old time, a lad in the employ of a farmer who occupied one of the homesteads was sent to our village to procure some little household necessaries from the shop. Dark

4

night had set in by the time he had reached Sandhill;
on his way home, when half way down the steep road,
the boy heard some one say, "I'm for Portallow-green."
"As you are going my way," thought he, "I may as well
have your company;" and he waited for a repetition of the
voice, intending to hail it. "I'm for Portallow-green," was
repeated after a short interval. "I'm for Portallow-green,"
shouted the boy. Quick as thought he found himself on
the green, surrounded by a throng of little laughing piskies.
They were, however, scarcely settled before the cry was
heard from several tiny voices, "I'm for Seaton-beach," —
a fine expanse of sand on the coast between this place and
Plymouth, at the distance of seven miles. Whether he was
charmed by his brief taste of pisky society, or taken with
their pleasant mode of travelling, is not stated; but, instead
of turning his pockets inside out, as many would have done,
he immediately rejoined, "I'm for Seaton-beach." Off he
was whisked, and in a moment found himself on Seaton-
beach. After they had for a while "danced their ringlets
to the whistling winds," the cry was changed to "I'm for
the king of France's cellar," and, strange to say, he offered
no objection even to so long a journey. "I'm for the king
of France's cellar," shouted the adventurous youth as he
dropped his parcel on the beach not far from the edge of
the tide. Immediately he found himself in a spacious
cellar, engaged with his mysterious companions in tasting
the richest of wines. They then passed through grand
rooms fitted up with a splendour which quite dazzled the
lad. In one apartment the tables were covered with fine
plate and rich viands, as if in expectation of a feast.
Though in the main an honest lad, he could not resist the
temptation to take away with him some memorial of his
travels, and he pocketed one of the rich silver goblets which
stood on the table. After a very short stay the word was
raised, "I'm for Seaton-beach," which being repeated by
the boy, he was taken back as quickly as he went, and
luckily reached the beach in time to save his parcel from
the flowing tide. The next destination was Portallow-

green, where the piskies left our wondering traveller, who reached home, delivered his parcel of groceries, and received a compliment from the good wife for his dispatch. "You'd say so, if you only know'd where I've been," said he; "I've been wi' the piskies to Seaton-beach, and I've been to the king o' France's house, and all in five minutes." The farmer stared and expressed an opinion that the boy was *mazed*. "I thought you'd say I was mazed, so I brort (brought) away this mug to show vor et," he replied, producing the goblet. The farmer and his family examined it, wondered at it, and finished by giving a full belief to the boy's strange story. The goblet is unfortunately not now to be produced for the satisfaction of those who may still doubt; but we are assured that it remained the property of the lad's family for generations after.

The Pisky Threshers. — The next legend, though connected by us with a particular farm-house in the neighbourhood, is of much wider fame, and well illustrates the capriciousness of their tempers, and shows that the little folk are easily offended by an offer of reward, however delicately tendered.

Long, long ago, before threshing-machines were thought of, the farmer who resided at C., in going to his barn one day, was surprised at the extraordinary quantity of corn that had been threshed during the previous night, as well as puzzled to discover the mysterious agency by which it was effected. His curiosity led him to inquire into the matter; so at night, when the moon was up, he crept stealthily to the barn-door; and looking through a chink, saw a little fellow, clad in a very tattered suit of green, wielding the "dreshel" (flail) with astonishing vigour, and beating the floor with blows so rapid that the eye could not follow the motions of the implement. The farmer slunk away unperceived, and crept to bed; where he lay a long while awake, thinking in what way he could best show his gratitude to the pisky for such an important service. He came to the conclusion, at length, that, as the little fellow's clothes were getting very old and ragged, the gift of a new suit would be

a proper way to lessen the obligation ; and, accordingly, on the morrow he had a suit of green made of what was supposed to be the proper size, which he carried early in the evening to the barn, and left for the pisky's acceptance. At night, the farmer stole to the door again to see how his gift was taken. He was just in time to see the elf put on the suit; which was no sooner accomplished than, looking down on himself admiringly, he sung :—

> " Pisky fine, and pisky gay,
> Pisky now will fly away."

Or, according to other narrators :—

> " Pisky new coat, and pisky new hood,
> Pisky now will do no more good."

From that time the farmer received no assistance from the fairy flail.

Another story tells how the farmer, looking through the key-hole, saw two elves threshing lustily, now and then interrupting their work to say to each other, in the smallest falsetto voice: " I tweat, you tweat ? " The poor man, unable to contain his gratitude, incautiously thanked them through the key-hole ; when the spirits, who love to work or play, " unheard and unespied," instantly vanished, and have never since visited that barn.

They seem sometimes to have delighted in mischief for its own sake. Old Robin Hicks, who formerly lived in a house on the cliff, has more than once, on stormy winter nights, been alarmed at his supper by a voice sharp and shrill : " Robin ! Robin ! your boat is adrift." Loud was the laughter and the *tacking* of hands when they succeeded in luring Robin as far as the quay, where the boat was lying safely at her moorings.

The Fisherman and the Piskies.—John Taprail, long since dead, moored his boat one evening beside a barge of much larger size, in which his neighbour John Rendle traded between this place and Plymouth ; and as the wind, though gusty, was not sufficient to cause any apprehension, he went to bed and slept soundly. In the middle of the night he was awoke by a voice from without bidding him get up, and " shift his rope over Rendle's," as his boat was in considerable danger. Now, as all Taprail's capital was invested in his boat and gear, we may be sure that he was not long in putting on his sea-clothes, and going to its rescue. To his great chagrin, he found that a joke had been played upon him, for the boat and barge were both riding quietly at their ropes. On his way back again, when within a few yards of his home, he observed a crowd of the little people congregated under the shelter of a boat that was lying high and dry on the beach. They were sitting in a semicircle, holding their hats towards one of their number, who was engaged in distributing a heap of money, pitching a gold piece into each hat in succession, after the manner in which cards are dealt. Now John had a covetous heart; and the sight of so much cash made him forget the respect due to an assembly of piskies, and that they are not slow to punish any intrusion on their privacy ; so he crept slyly towards them, hidden by the boat, and, reaching round, managed to introduce his hat without exciting any notice. When the heap was getting low, and Taprail was awaking to the dangers of detection, he craftily withdrew his hat and made off with the prize. He had got a fair start, before the trick was discovered; but the defrauded piskies were soon on his heels, and he barely managed to reach his house and to close the door upon his pursuers. So narrow indeed was his escape, that he had left the tails of his sea-coat in their hands. Such is the evidently imperfect version of an old legend, as it is remembered by the fishermen of the present generation. We may suppose that John Taprail's door had a key-hole ; and there would have been poetical justice in the story, if the elves had compelled the fraudulent fisherman to turn his hat or pocket inside out.

Our legend of the pisky midwife is so well related by Mrs. Bray, that it need not again be told, the only material difference being that in our story it was the accidental application to her eye of the soap with which she was washing the baby, that opened to her the secrets of fairy land. (Abridged by Keightley, *Fairy Myth.*, Bohn's edition, p. 301.)

I have been unable to discover any traces of a belief in the existence of water-spirits. An old man was accustomed to relate that he saw, one stormy day, a woman, with long dank locks, sitting on the rocks in Talland Bay, and apparently weeping; and that, on his approach, she slid into the water and disappeared. This story is easily accounted for by supposing that he saw a seal (an animal that occasionally frequents that locality), the long hair being an allowable embellishment. Our fishermen talk of " mermaids ; " and the egg-cases of the rays and sharks, which sometimes strew our beaches, are popularly called "mermaids purses ; " but it is extremely doubtful whether these notions are a part of our old mythology.

Besides the piskies, but of a widely different character and origin, are the spectre-huntsman and his pack, now known as "the Devil and his Dandy-dogs." The genius of the tradition is essentially Scandinavian, and reminds us of the grim sights and terrible sounds which affright the belated peasant in the forests of the north. The tradition has become variously altered in its passage down to us, but it still retains enough of the terrible to mark its derivation. " The Devil and his Dandy-dogs " frequent our bleak and dismal moors on tempestuous nights, and are more rarely heard and seen in the cultivated districts by the coast, where they assume a less frightful character. They are most commonly seen by those who are out at night on wicked errands, and woe betide the wretch who crosses their path. A very interesting legend is told here, though it has reference to the wild moorland district far inland.

The Devil and his Dandy-dogs. — A poor herdsman was journeying homeward across the moors one windy night, when he heard at a distance among the tors the baying of hounds, which he soon recognised as the dismal chorus of the dandy-dogs. It was three or four miles to his home ; and, very much alarmed, he hurried onward as fast as the treacherous nature of the soil and the uncertainty of the path would allow ; but, alas ! the melancholy yelping of the hounds, and the dismal halloa of the hunter came nearer and nearer. After a considerable run, they had so gained upon him, that on looking back — oh, horror ! — he could distinctly see hunter and dogs. The former was terrible to look at, and had the usual complement of *saucer-eyes,* horns, and tail accorded by common consent to the legendary devil. He was black, of course, and carried in his hand a long hunting-pole. The dogs, a numerous pack, blackened the small patch of moor that was visible ; each snorting fire, and uttering a yelp of an indescribably frightful tone. No cottage, rock, or tree was near to give the herdsman shelter, and nothing apparently remained to him but to abandon himself to their fury, when a happy thought suddenly flashed upon him, and suggested a resource. Just as they were about to rush upon him, he fell on his knees in prayer. There was strange power in the holy words he uttered : for immediately, as if resistance had been offered, the hell-hounds stood at bay, howling more dismally than ever ; and the hunter shouted " Bo shrove ! " " which," says my informant, " means, in the old language, *the boy prays.*" At which they all drew off on some other pursuit, and disappeared.

This ghastly apparition loses much of its terrible character as we approach more thickly populated districts, and our stories are very tame after this legend of the Moors. Many of the tales which I have heard are so well attested, that there is some reason to conclude that the narrators have really seen a pack of *fairies* (the local name, it is necessary to add, of the weasel) ; of which it is well known that they hunt gregariously at night-time, and, when so engaged, do not scruple to attack man.

We have no Duergar, Troll, or swart fairy of the mine ; for ours is not a mining neighbourhood, and our hills have no fissures or caverns such as they delight to haunt.

Another object of superstition among our fishermen is the *white hare,* a being resembling the *létiche.* It frequents our quays by night, and is quite harmless, except that its appearance is held to predict a storm.

Very palpable modifications of the old creed are to be noticed in the account of the " Devil and his Dandy-dogs," as well as in the opinion commonly held, that the fairy ranks are recruited by infants who are allowed to die without the rite of baptism.

It is with a feeling of jealousy that we first make the discovery, that the familiar tales which we have been taught from earliest days to associate with particular localities are told in foreign tongues by far-off firesides. But they soon assume a loftier interest when we become awake to their significance ; and find that in them may be traced, as an eminent antiquary remarks,—

" The early formation of nations, their identity or analogy, their changes, as well as the inner texture of the national character, more deeply than in any other circumstances, even in language itself."— Wright, *Essays on Subjects connected with the Literature, &c., of England in the Middle Ages.*

The stories of the " Pisky Threshers " and the " Pisky Midwife" frequently occur, with variations, in the legends which Keightley has so industriously collected in his learned and interesting *Fairy Mythology ;* but the " Voyage of the Piskies " and " The Fishermen and the Piskies " are not so common. The former will, however, remind the reader of the adventures of Lord Duffers, as given by Aubrey. In Mackie's *Castles, Palaces, and Prisons of Mary Queen of Scots,* a similar tale is told of a butler in the house of Monteith ; with this difference, that the traveller had witches for his companions, and a bulrush for his nag.

Witchcraft, &c. — The belief in witchcraft holds its ground very firmly, and of all superstitions it will probably be the last to die out, since, to mention no other influence, the inductive process of reasoning will never be a popular one ; and there will always be a greater number who, too impatient to question the material, hastily resort to the spiritual for an explanation of all phenomena, down to the creakings and oscillations of tables. Many strange natural coincidences are occurring daily, which to minds not over-nice about distinctions between *post* and *propter*, have all the relationship of cause and effect.

The notion that mysterious compacts are formed between evil spirits and wicked men has become almost obsolete. In the present day such a bargain is rarely suspected, and there are few found hardy enough to avow themselves parties to so unholy a transaction. One instance occurs to my memory of a poor unhappy fellow who pretended, in vulgar parlance, to have sold himself to the devil, and was accordingly regarded by his neighbours as a miracle of impiety. He was not, however, actively vicious, never being known to use his supernatural powers of ill-doing to the detriment of others, except, indeed (and they were the only occasions upon which he is said to have openly asked the foul fiend's assistance), when the depth of his potations had not left him enough to pay the reckoning. He was then accustomed to hold his hat up the chimney, and demand money, which was promptly showered down into it. The coin so obtained the landlord invariably refused with a shudder, and was glad to get quit of him on these terms. This compact with the spirit of evil is now but vaguely suspected as the secret of the witch's power.

The faculty of witchcraft is held to be hereditary, and it is not the least cruel of the effects of this horrible creed, that many really good-natured souls have on this account been kept aloof by their neighbours, and rendered miserable by being ever the object of unkind suspicions. When communication with such persons cannot be avoided, their ill-will is deprecated by a slavish deference. If met on the highway, care is taken to pass them on the right hand.

Witches are supposed to have the power of changing their shape and resuming it again at will. A large hare which haunted this neighbourhood had on numberless occasions baffled the hounds, or carried off, unhurt, incredible quantities of shot. One luckless day it crossed the path of a party of determined sportsmen, who followed it for many weary miles, and fired several rounds with the usual want of success. Before relinquishing the chase, one of them, who considered the animal as something beyond an ordinary hare, suggested the trial of silver bullets, and, accordingly, silver coins were beaten into slugs for this purpose. The hare was again seen, fired at, and, this time, wounded, though not so effectually as to prevent its running round the brow of the hill, and disappearing among the rocks. In searching for the hare, they discovered instead old Molly, crouched under a shelving rock, panting and flushed by the long chase. From that day forward she had a limp in her gait.

The toad and the black cat are the most usual attendants of the witch, or rather the form her imps most commonly assume. The appearance of a toad on the doorstep is taken for a certain sign that the house is under evil influence, and the poor reptile is put to some frightfully barbarous death.

The most common results of the witch's malice, or, as it is termed, *the ill-wish*, are misfortunes in business, diseases of an obstinate and deadly character in the family, or among the cattle. The cow refuses "to give down her milk," the butter is spoilt in making, or the household is tormented by a visitation in incredible numbers of those animalcules said " to be familiar to man, and to signify love." There are a hundred other ways in which the evil influence may be manifested.

When witchcraft is suspected, the person *overlooked* has immediate recourse to the *conjurer*, the very bad representative of the astrologer of a former age. The conjurer is an important character in our village. He is resorted to by despairing lovers ; he counsels those who are under the evil eye, and discloses the whereabouts of stolen goods. His answers, too, are given with true oracular ambiguity. " Own horn eat own corn " was his reply to a person who consulted him about the disappearance of various little household articles. When appealed to in cases of suspected witchcraft, the certainty of weird influence is proved beyond doubt, and the first letter of the witch's name, or description of her person is given, or even, so it is said, her bodily presence shown in a mirror. I know but little of the incantations practised on these occasions.

The certainty of the ill-wish being thus established, and the person of the witch fixed on, the remembrance of some past "difference" or quarrel places the matter beyond doubt. This mode of proceeding to a conclusion is truly and quaintly described by old Dr. Harsenet. "Beware, look about you, my neighbours. If any of you have a sheep sick of the giddies, or a hog of the mumps, or a horse of the staggers, or a knavish boy of the school, or an idle girl of the wheel, or a young drab of the sullens, and hath not fat enough for her porrage, or butter enough for her bread, and she hath a little help of the epilepsy, or cramp, to teach her to roll her eyes, wry her mouth, gnash her teeth, startle with her body, hold her arms and hands stiff, &c. And then when an old Mother Nobs hath by chance called her ' idle young housewife,' or bid the devil scratch, then no doubt but Mother Nobs is the witch, and the young girl is owl-blasted." (*Declaration of Popish Impostures, quoted by Hutchinson.*)

One of the various methods of dissolving the spell is now resorted to. It is a belief that the power for evil ceases the moment blood is drawn from the witch, and this is now and then tried, as in a late instance where a man was summoned before the bench of magistrates and fined for having assaulted the plaintiff and scratched her with a pin. When an ox or other beast has died in consequence of the ill-wish, it is usual to take out the heart, stick it over with pins and nails, and roast it before the fire until the pins and nails have one by one dropped out of it; during which process the witch is supposed to be suffering in mysterious sympathy with the wasting heart. There are many stories told of how the wicked woman has been driven by these means to confess, and to loose the family from the spell. Recourse is sometimes had to measures of a less delicate description. When the friendly parasites become unpleasantly numerous

G 2

15

it was, not long since, the custom to send a friend, or even the town crier, to shout near the door of the witch, " Take back your flock! take back your flock!" a ceremony which was said to be followed by an abatement of the inconvenience. The wiser method of preventing spells is very often taken, and the house and all it contains are protected by the nailing of a horse-shoe over the centre of the doorway. There are few farm-houses without it, and scarcely a boat or vessel puts to sea without this talisman. Another preventive of great fame is the mountain-ash, or *care*, of which more hereafter.

Besides the witch and the conjurer, we have yet another and more pleasing character to mention, namely the *charmer*. She is generally an elderly woman of good reputation, and supposed to be gifted with supernatural power, which she exercises for good. By her incantations and ceremonies she stops blood, cures inflamed eyes, and the erysipelas, *vulgo vocato, wild-fire.* I know but little of her doings, except that she is too much given to make frequent and vain use of sacred names in her verses. The following is one of her many charms, good for an inflammation : —

> " There were two angels came from the east;
> One brought fire the other frost.
> Out fire! in frost!
> In the name of " &c.

I shall finish this note by transcribing an original letter dated Septr. ye 14th, 1696, and addressed by Blackburne (? Archdeacon) to the Bishop of Exeter of that date. It is interesting, and comes in appropriately as illustrative of witchcraft in the West of England. The case is mentioned by Hutchinson, who gives some details which do not differ from those here given, and remarks that "no inconvenience hath followed from her acquittal." (*Historical Essay*, p. 612. 2nd edit.)

" My Most Hon^d. Lord,

Y^r Lordship was pleas'd to command me by Mustion to attend the tryal of y^e witch, and give you some account of it. It was thus :

Elizabeth Horner, alias Turner, was arraigned on three several inditements for murthering Alice, the daughter of Thomas and Elizabeth Bovet, and for pining and laming Sarah and Mary, daughters of ye same Thomas and Elizabeth Bovet.

The evidence given wch was anything material was this: — Thomas Bovet, the father, swears that Alice the youngest of ye three daughters, being about four years old was taken very ill in her belly, &c., that physitiens cou'd see no natural cause of her illness, and y^t she died in five days. That Mary was so taken likewise. Her body strangely distorted, and her legs twisted like the screw of a gun, that she wou'd often go wth her eyes shut into the fire, and say that Bett Horner drove her in: continued thus about seven weeks. She was about ten years old.

That Sarah, nine years old, was taken after the same manner, — complained of being scratch't in bed by a cat wch she said was Bett Horner, whom she described exactly in the apparel she had on, tho' the child had not seen her in six months before.

That after her imprisonment they were both tormented by pinching and biting, all ye time crying out stil on Bett Horner, at present the prints of pinches and markes of teeth appearing on their arms and cheeks (this point attested also by Justice Auchester who was wth the children at ye time). That they would vomit pins and stones, two crooked pins came away in Sarah's water. Sarah cry'd out, the witch had put a pin into her, the point of one appeared just under the skin, and at last it came out upon her middle finger; cry'd out of being struck by the witch wth a stick, the mark of which stroke appear'd at the time upon her ankle. Sarah said that Bett Horner told her how she kill'd Alice by squeezing her breath out of her body, and that she had a teat on her left shoulder which was suck't by toads.

Elizabeth Bovet, the mother, depos'd in like manner concerning Alice, who continued ill five days, and so dy'd, crying out, — Why doe you kill me. That Sarah and Mary

G 3

were taken ill alternately, not able to say their prayers, saying they were threatened by the witch, if they shou'd doe it, to be served by her as Alice was, and that she made 'em swear and curse. That they were both of late very hungry and being ask'd why they were so, they said the head of Bett Horner came off of her body and went into their belly, which wou'd, when they said so appear to be prodigiously swell'd, and the swelling abate all of a sudden, when they said it was gone out of 'em again.

That Sarah walk't up a wall nine foot high four or five times backwards and forwards, her face and forepart of her body parallel to the ceiling of y\ :superscript{e} room, saying at the time that Bett Horner carry'd her up.

The children were also produced in court, who gave the same account sensibly enough, Mary adding further that she saw Bett Horner in her full shape, playing with a toad in a basin, and leaving it suck her at a nipple between her breast and shoulder.

Alice Osborne swore that she threaten'd her upon refusing her some barm. She afterwards found a vessel, after she had wash't it for brewing, fill'd full of drink which they threw away, and then brewing and filling y\ :superscript{e} vessel with drink, in four or five days, neither she, nor her husband having drawn any, she found it quite empty and as dry as if no drink had ever been in it. That Bett Horner threatened her husband saying, Thou hast children as well as others, and if I come home again, I'll mind some of 'em.

John Fursey depos'd to his seeing her three nights together upon a large down in the same place as if rising out of the ground.

Margaret Armiger depos'd that on y\ :superscript{e} Saturday before the tryal, when the witch was in prison, she met her in the country at about twenty feet distance from her.

Mary Stevens depos'd she took a red-hot nail, and drove it into the witch's left foot-step, upon which she went lame, and being search'd her leg and foot appear'd to be red and fiery, that she continued so four or five days, when she pull'd up the nail again, and then the witch was well. This is what was most material against her. The witch deny'd all, shew'd her shoulder bare in court, when there appear'd nothing but a kind of mole or wart, as it seem'd to me. She said the Lord's prayer, stopping a little at *forgive us our trespasses*, but recovered and went on, and she repeated the Creed without a fault.

My Lord Chief Justice, by his questions and manner of hemming up the evidence seem'd to me to believe nothing of witchery at all, and to disbelieve the fact of walking up the wall, which was sworn by the mother.

My Lord,
Y^r Lp^s Most Oblig'd and
Most obedient humble Serv
BLACKBURNE."

Charms, Omens, &c.—The domestic treatment of disease among our poor consists chiefly of charms and ceremonies; and even when material remedies are employed, as much importance is attached to the rites which attend their employment as to the agents used. In many cases we may notice remnants of the old doctrine of signatures, and the idea of sympathies and antipathies between separate and dissimilar bodies. In the cure of hæmorrhages, the preference is given to medicines of a bright red colour; and saffron-water, the brightest-coloured decoction they are acquainted with, is administered to throw out eruptions of the skin. The nettle-rash is treated by copious draughts of nettle-tea. The fisherman, whose hand is wounded by a hook, is very careful to preserve that hook from rust during the healing of the wound.

The following instances will illustrate the superstitious character of the household medicine of the poorer of our population :—

If the infant suffers from the *thrush*, it is taken, fasting, on three following mornings, " to have its mouth blown into " by a posthumous child. If afflicted with the hooping cough, it is fed with the bread and butter of a family the heads of which bear respectively the names John and Joan—a

G 4

serious thing for the poor couple in time of an epidemic. Or if a piebald horse is to be found in the country, the child is taken to it, and passed thrice under its belly. The mere possession of such a beast confers the power of curing this disease. The owner of a piebald horse states that he has frequently been stopped on the road by anxious mothers, who inquire of him in a casual way, what is good for the hooping cough; and the thing he mentioned, however inappropriate or absurd, was held to be a certain remedy in that particular case.

The passing of children through holes in the earth, rocks, or trees, once an established rite, is still practised in various parts of Cornwall. With us, boils are cured by creeping on the hands and knees beneath a bramble which has grown into the soil at both ends. Children affected with hernia are still passed through a slit in an ash sapling before sunrise fasting; after which the slit portions are bound up, and as they unite so the malady is cured. The ash is indeed a tree of many virtues: venomous reptiles are never known to rest under its shadow, and a single blow from an ash stick is instant death to an adder; struck by a bough of any other tree, the reptile is said to retain marks of life until the sun goes down. The antipathy of the serpent to the ash is a very old popular fallacy. (Pliny, *Hist. Mundi*, lib. xvi.)

The mountain ash, or *care*, has still greater repute among our country-folk in the curing of ills arising from supernatural as well as ordinary causes. It is dreaded by evil spirits; it renders null the spells of the witch, and has many other wonderful properties. The countryman will carry for years a piece of the wood in his pocket as a charm against ill-wish, or as a remedy for his rheumatism. If his cow is out of health, and he suspects her to be *overlooked*, away he runs to the nearest wood and brings home bunches of care, which he suspends over her stall, and wreathes round her horns; after which he considers her safe.

Boys, when stung by nettles, have great faith in the antidotal properties of the dock; and whilst rubbing it into the

21

part in pain, repeat the words, " Out nettle, in dock—nettle, nettle, stung me."

The cures for warts are many and various. A piece of flesh is taken secretly, and rubbed over the warts ; it is then buried ; and as the flesh decays, the warts vanish. Or some mysterious vagrant desires them to be carefully counted, and marking the number on the inside of his hat, leaves the neighbourhood—when the warts also disappear.

There are a few animals the subject of superstitious veneration, and a much greater number whose actions are supposed to convey intimations of the future. In some instances it would seem that they are considered more in the light of *cause* than *prognostic ;* yet as the doctrine of fatalism, in a restricted sense, runs through the popular belief, we may consider the conduct of the inhospitable housewife who drives off the cock that crows on the door-step, thereby warning her of the approach of strangers, as only a fresh illustration of the very old fallacy, that the way to avert the prediction is to silence the prophet. Here are some of our superstitions connected with animals, &c. : —

The howling of dogs, the continued croaking of ravens over a house, and the ticking of the death-watch, portend death. The magpie is a bird of good or ill omen, according to the number seen at a time : —

> " One for sorrow ; two for mirth ;
> Three for a wedding ; four for death."

A crowing hen is a bird of ill luck. An old proverb in use here says : —

> " A whistling woman, and a crowing hen, are two of the unluckiest things under the sun."

The first is always reproved, and the latter got rid of without loss of time. Pluquet, in his book on the superstitions of Bayeux, gives this identical proverb : —

> " Une poule qui chante le coq, et une fille qui siffle, portent malheur dans la maison."

22

If, on the first hearing the cuckoo, the sounds proceed from the right, it signifies that you will be prosperous ; or, to use the language of my informant, a country lad, " You will go vore in the world ; " if from the left, ill-luck is before you. Children are frequently heard to hail the cuckoo in a verse which, as it has recently appeared in " N. & Q." I shall not repeat, except the former part of the second quatrain, which is a pretty variation from the commoner version : —

> " *He sucks the sweet flowers,*
> To make his voice clear."

Particular honour is paid to the robin and the wren. A local distich says :—

> " He that hurts a robin or a wren
> Will never prosper sea nor land."

This gives them a protection which the most mischievous urchin never dares to violate.

It is a very prevalent belief that a bed-pillow, stuffed with the feathers of wild birds, renders painful and prolonged the departure of the dying. Death is also thought to be delayed until the ebb of the tide.

The killing the first adder you see predicts that you will triumph over your enemies. The slough of an adder, hung on the rafters, preserves the house against fire.

Our forefathers appear to have been among those who considered bees as possessing a portion " divinæ mentis : " for there is a degree of deference yet paid to them, that would scarcely be offered to beings endowed with only ordinary animal instinct. On the death of a relative, the bees are acquainted of the event by moving the hive, or putting it in mourning by attaching a piece of black cloth or crape to it. The sale of bees is a very unlucky proceeding ; and they are generally transferred to another owner, with the tacit understanding that a bushel of corn (the constant value of a swarm) is to be given in return. In cases of death, the in-door plants are also put in black ; for, if this is omitted, they soon droop and die.

The cricket is a bringer of good luck, and its departure from a house is a sign of coming misfortune.

Amongst the omens believed in, or existing in proverbs, I may farther mention, that the breaking of a looking-glass entails " seven years' trouble, but no want ;" that the dirgeful singing of children portends a funeral. There is scarcely a sensation but has its meaning. If the left palm itches, you will have to pay money; if the right, to receive. If the knee itches, you will kneel in a strange church; if the sole of the foot, you will walk over strange ground ; if the elbow, you will sleep with a strange bed-fellow. If the ear tingles, you will hear sudden news. If you shiver, some one is walking over the spot destined to be your grave. If the cheek burns, some one is talking scandal of you. I have frequently heard these lines spoken by the person whose cheek is burning :—

> " Right cheek !—left cheek ! why do you burn?
> Cursed be she that doth me any harm :
> If she be a maid, let her be slaid ;
> If she be a widow, long let her mourn :
> But if it be my own true love—burn, cheek, burn ! "

THOMAS Q. COUCH.

Cornwall.

PIXIES OR PISKIES.

At Chudleigh Rocks I was told, a few weeks ago, by the old man who acts as guide to the caves, of a recent instance of a man's being pixy-led. In going home, full of strong drink, across the hill above the cavern called the " Pixies' Hole," on a moonlit night, he heard sweet music, and was led into the whirling dance by the " good folk," who kept on spinning him without mercy, till he fell down "in a swoon."

On " coming to himself," he got up and found his way home, where he "took to his bed, and never left it again, but died a little while after," the victim (I suppose) of *delirium tremens,* or some such disorder, the incipient symptoms of which his haunted fancy turned into the sweet music in the night wind and the fairy revel on the heath. In the tale I have above given he persisted (said the old man) when the medical attendant who was called in inquired of him the symptoms of his illness. This occurrence happened, I understood, very recently, and was told to me in perfect good faith.

I have just been told of a man who several years ago lost his way on Whitchurch Down, near Tavistock. The farther he went the farther he had to go; but happily calling to mind the antidote " in such case made and provided," he turned his coat inside out, after which he had no difficulty in finding his way. " He was supposed," adds my informant, " to be pisky-led."

About ten miles from Launceston, on the Bodmin road (or at least in that direction) is a large piece of water called Dosmere (pronounced Dosmery) Pool. A tradition of the neighbourhood says that on the shores of this lonely mere the ghosts of bad men are ever employed in binding the sand " in bundles with *beams* of the same" (a local word meaning *bands,* in Devonshire called *beans;* as *hay-beans,*

and in this neighbourhood hay-*beams*, for hay-bands). These ghosts, or some of them, were driven out (they say "*horse-whipped* out," at any rate exorcised in some sort) "by the parson" from Launceston. H. G. T.—(Vol. ii. p. 511.)
Launceston.

An old woman, the wife of a respectable farmer at a place called "Colmans," in the parish of Werrington, near Launceston, has frequently told my informant of a "piskey" (for *so*, and not *pixy*, the creature is called *here*, as well as in parts of Devon) which frequently *made its appearance* in the form of a small child in the kitchen of the farm-house, where the inmates were accustomed to set a little stool for it. It would do a good deal of household work, but if the hearth and the chimney corner were not kept neatly swept, it would pinch the maid. The piskey would often come into the kitchen and sit on its little stool before the fire, so that the old lady had many opportunities of seeing it. Indeed it was a familiar guest in the house for many months. At last it left the family under these circumstances. One evening it was sitting on the stool as usual, when it suddenly started, looked up and said,—

> "Piskey fine, and Piskey gay,
> Now, Piskey! run away!"

and vanished; after which it never appeared again. This distich is the first utterance of a piskey I have heard.

It is worth notice that the people here seem to entertain no doubt as to the identity of piskies and fairies. Indeed I am told, that the old woman before mentioned called her guest indifferently "piskey" or "fairy."

The country people in this neighbourhood sometimes put a prayer-book under a child's pillow as a charm to keep away the piskies. I am told that a poor woman near Launceston was fully persuaded that one of her children was taken away and a pisky substituted, the disaster being caused by the absence of the prayer-book on one particular night. This story reminds me of the "killcrop."

H. G. T.—(Vol. ii. p. 475.)

In reference to your correspondent H. G. T.'s article on Pixies, allow me to say that I have read the distich which he quotes in a tale to the following effect :

In one of the southern counties of England — (all the pixey tales which I have heard or read have their seat laid in the south of England)—there lived a lass who was courted and wed by a man who, after marriage, turned out to be a drunkard, neglecting his work, which was that of threshing, thereby causing his pretty wife to starve. But after she could bear this no longer, she dressed herself in her husband's clothes (whilst he slept off the effects of his drunkenness), and went to the barn to do her husband's work. On the morning of the second day, when she went to the barn, she found a large pile of corn thrashed, which she had not done ; and so she found, for three or four days, her pile of corn doubled. One night she determined to watch and see who did it, and carrying her intention into practice, she saw a little pixey come into the barn to a tiny flail, with which he set to work so vigorously that he soon thrashed a large quantity. During his work he sang,

> " Little Pixey, fair and slim,
> Without a rag to cover him."

The next day the good woman made a complete suit of miniature clothes, and hung them up behind the barn door, and watched to see what *pixey* would do. I forgot to mention that he hung his flail behind the door when he had done with it.

At the usual time the pixey came to work, went to the door to take down his flail, and saw the suit of clothes, took them down, and put them on him, and surveyed himself with a satisfied air, and sang

> "Pixey fine, and pixey gay,
> Pixey now must fly away."

It then flew away, and she never saw it more.

In this tale the word was invariably spelt " pixey."

TYSIL.

Pixies.—The *puckie*-stone is a rock above the Teign, near

Chagford.   In the *Athenæum* I mentioned the rags in which the pixies generally appear.   In *A Narrative of some strange Events that took place in Island Magee and Neighbourhood in* 1711, is this description of a spirit that troubled the house of Mr. James Hattridge :

"About the 11th of December, 1710, when the aforesaid Mrs. Hattridge was sitting at the kitchen-fire, in the evening, before daylight going, a little boy (as she and the servants supposed) came in and sat down beside her, having an old black bonnet on his head, with short black hair, a half-worn blanket about him, trailing on the ground behind him, and a *torn* black vest under it.   He seemed to be about ten or twelve years old, but he still covered his face, holding his arm with a piece of the blanket before it.   She desired to see his face, but he took no notice of her.   Then she asked him several questions; viz. if he was cold or hungry?   If he would have any meat?   Where he came from, and where he was going?   To which he made no answer, but getting up, danced very nimbly, leaping higher than usual, and then ran out of the house as far as the end of the garden, and sometimes into the cowhouse, the servants running after him to see where he would go, but soon lost sight of him; but when they returned he would be close after them in the house, which he did above a dozen of times.   At last the little girl, seeing her master's dog coming in, said, ' Now my master is coming he will take a course with this troublesome creature,' upon which he immediately went away, and troubled them no more till the month of February, 1711."

This costume is appropriate enough for an Irish spirit; but there may possibly be some connexion with the ragged clothes of the Pixies. (Comp. " Tateman," *Deutsche Mythol.*, p. 470. ; and Canciani's note "De Simulachris de Pannis factis," *Leges Barbar.*, iii. p. 168. ; *Indic. Superst.*) The common story of Brownie and his clothes is, I suppose, connected.

In some parts of Devonshire the pixies are called " derricks." In Cornwall it is believed that wherever the pixies are fond of resorting, the depths of the earth are rich in metal. Very many mines have been discovered by their singing.   R. J. K.—(Vol. ii. p. 514.)

29

THOMAS TONKIN ON PISKIES, &c., c. 1727.

Tonkin *(Natural History MS.,* pp. 10—11*)* writes as follows :—

"Many strange stories we have, more especially among the miners, of Fairies, or, as they call them, Piskys, Small People, &c. ; of their discovering Mines to them, playing on Musick very sweetly in them, &c., Dancing in Rings and Circles, from whence come the many bare rings and circles which we see in many places, particularly one in a field of my own on Trevaunance, called The Rose Field, where I have been told of above 20 several appearances of them even in the day time. But as I look upon them all as perfect whimsies and dreams, I shall say no more of them." [Here he refers to botanical works proving the fungous origin of such rings].

"I remember that about 40 years since, *viz.*, about 1687, one Agnes Martin, of St. Agnes, pretended that she had been carried away by these Small People, and gave a long account of her living among them, &c., and that her employment was to look after the children. I have often discours'd her about it since that time, she being now dead, and by the best conjectures that I could make she was carried away by a gang of Gipsies (for she was certainly wanting several years, and no one could tell what was become of her, till she was accidentally met with in a Fair and brought home), and being very young, not above 7 or 8 years of age, carried about from place to place generally by night, &c. ; she verily believed the tale she told, and that she lived with them underground, was very well treated by them, and (no doubt) had this story put into her head by them. I mention this little story as being within my own knowledge, and not unknown, neither, to many people still living, who have had it from her own mouth : and also for that I verily believe most of these tales so rife among us have as little foundation, if as much as this."

Tonkin's explanation, that all Agnes Martin's tale was put into her head by gipsies, seems quite unnecessary when one knows that it was generally believed at the time that young girls might be taken away by the Small People to look after their children. In Bottrell's stories, " Cherry of Zennor " in Hunt, and " The Fairy Master " in his own book, we have semi-rationalised versions of the same tale as lived in imagination by a girl who, going down for the first time from a wild moorland parish into the richer " Low Countries " about Penzance, fancies herself walking into a Fairyland, while her new master's house, with its waxed floors, marble busts and harpsichord, takes on the likeness of a fairy palace filled with marvels. No girl would be likely to imagine herself the heroine of such a fairy-tale, however, unless the tale itself had often been told to her before ; the intercourse of Anne Jefferies with the fairies was apparently well known throughout 17th-century Cornwall, people coming to her to be healed from as far off as the Land's End, and Agnes Martin, whether we believe that she really lived with the Small People or not, would probably have taken the possibility of such things happening as beyond doubt. Had Tonkin given us more of her "long account of her living among them, &c.," we might have been able to judge how much the seeing of fact through the glamour of an old tale had to do with them.

R.M.N.

————

31

HORSE RIDING PISKIES.

On the moors in the neighbourhood of Summercourt in the old days, it was frequently found that when the ponies and colts were rounded up just before Summercourt fair and other times that their manes were badly tangled up and on looking closely into the manes, it was found that they were often looped up in such a fashion as to appear very much like stirrups for little folk. On the Goss Moors, it was always said that the Piskies could come up to the sides of the ponies at night and mount them by these stirrups and would ride these half-wild animals over the moors and downs at a furious pace. In fact it was often said by the Moormen that they had seen them doing it. It sometime happened, however, that the animals would get their hind legs entangled in the long loops of the manes and be thrown badly—sometimes being unable to rise for a long time.

Piskies did not however, confine their exercises to the moorland, for often in the old days it was no unusual thing for a Cornish house-wife to rise in the morning to get "Maister's breakfast" and to find the kitchen cleaned and the pots and pans and stove shining as if the day's work were done and to know that none other than the Piskies had been doing their "good turn." The reason these nocturnal operations ceased in the Duchy was because of the inquisitiveness of people after the passing of the 1870 Education Act. They watched to see how it was done and the little folk didn't like it and so forgot to drop cards on inquisitive people who didn't know when they were well off.

"THICKY LAST OL' MOON WASN'T KIND."

The moon is the subject of much concern in Cornwall. It is most unlucky to see her through glass. On the appearance of the new moon, everyone is anxious to see her and households will empty on her appearance in order to obtain good luck for the month. The best way to ensure good luck is immediately on sight of her to turn over all the money in your pockets. Polite old ladies in the past always used to curtsey to her. As to the fate of the weather during the lunar month, that depends on the position of the moon. If she lies on her back, then she is carrying the rain. A Summercourt man would always observe after a wet month that "Thicky last old moon wasn't kind."

SUPERSTITION OF CORNISH MINERS.

SUPERSTITION OF THE CORNISH MINERS.

Mr. Kingsley records a superstition of the Cornish miners, which I have not seen noted elsewhere. In reply to the question, " What are the *Knockers?*" Tregarva answers :—

" They are *the ghosts,* the miners hold, *of the Old Jews that crucified our Lord, and were sent for slaves by the Roman emperors to work the mines :* and we find their old smelting-houses, which we call *Jews' houses,* and their blocks of the bottom of the great bogs, which we call *Jews' tin :* and then a town among us, too, which we call *Market Jew,* but the old name was *Marazion,* that means the Bitterness of Zion, they tell me; and bitter work it was for them no doubt, poor souls! We used to break into the old shafts and adits which they had made, and find old stags-horn pickaxes, that crumbled to pieces when we brought them to grass. And they say that if a man will listen of a still night about those old shafts, he may hear the ghosts of them at working, knocking, and picking, as clear as if there was a man at work in the next level."—*Yeast; a Problem :* Lond. 1851, p. 255.

Miners, as a class, are peculiarly susceptible of impressions of the unseen world, and the superstitions entertained by them in different parts of the world would form a curious volume. Is there any work on Cornish folk lore which alludes to this superstition respecting the Jews?

EIRIONNACH. — (Vol. viii. p. 7.)

I cannot find the information desired by your correspondent in the Cornish antiquaries, and have in vain consulted other works likely to explain this tradition; but the remarks now offered will perhaps be interesting in reference to the *nation* alluded to. The Carthaginians being of the same race, manners, and religion as the Phœnicians, there are no particular data by which we can ascertain the time of their first trading to the British coast for the commodity in such request among the traders of the East. The genius of Carthage being more martial than that of Tyre, whose object was more commerce than conquest, it is not improbable that the former might by force of arms have established a settlement in the Cassiterides, and by this means have secured that monopoly of tin which the Phœnicians and their colonies indubitably enjoyed for several centuries. Norden, in his *Antiquities of Cornwall,* mentions it as a tradition universally received by the inhabitants, that their tin mines were formerly wrought by the Jews. He adds that these old works are there at this day called Attal Sarasin, the ancient cast-off works of the Saracens, in which their tools are frequently found. Miners are not accustomed to be very accurate in distinguishing traders of foreign nations, and these Jews and Saracens have probably a reference to the old merchants from Spain and Africa; and those employed by them might possibly have been Jews escaped the horrors of captivity and the desolation which about that period befel their country.

" The Jews," says Whitaker (*Origin of Arianism*, p. 334.), " denominated themselves, and were denominated by the Britons of Cornwall, *Saracens,* as the genuine progeny of Sarah. The same name, no doubt, carried the same reference with it as borne by the genuine, and as usurped by the spurious, offspring of Abraham."

BIBLIOTHECAR. CHETHAM.—(Vol. viii. p. 215.)

CORNISH WITCHCRAFT

W. H. (for Bill) PAYNTER

MANY YEARS AGO, I set myself the task of collecting the superstitions and folklore associated with Cornwall. I realised that with the present generation probably all these relics of the past will disappear. I therefore set out on my so-called witch hunt.

It was not an easy task, however, for I soon discovered the difficulty in getting behind the scenes in order to find out as there appeared a subconsciousness that such dealings are unorthodox, and again there was the fear of ridicule.

Spells and magic, evil wishes and sudden cures are very near and potent things and to question their existence would be flying in the face of providence. Again, I frequently met with the remark that the Bible denouces witches, " Thou shalt not suffer a witch to live " says *Exodus* 22, 18, and time and time again, I was reminded of this by people who, to use their own words, " wish to get their own back after being bewitched or over-looked !

Others again reminded me that preacher John Wesley was a firm believer in ghosts and witches and insisted upon it years after all laws upon the subject had been repealed in this country.

It is interesting to note that although John Wesley's views on familiar spirits have been frequently alluded, as far as I am able to ascertain, no convincing statement has been published to show his actual attitude towards the question of witchcraft. Doubtless the Bible text, as well as convincing John Wesley served as the basis for many a witch hunt and bitter prosecution in the past.

Probably few people are aware how widespread was the belief, not a great many years ago, in charms and charmers and other superstitions or that there were witches in almost every village, shunned and dreaded by some who feared their supposed power to ill-wish those who offended them and sought out by others who wanted their aid to avert the evil eye or by their magic to remove spells already cast on them or their cattle by an ill-wisher who had over-looked them.

In my witch hunt, I covered the whole of Cornwall, visiting

parish by parish and came across numerous cases of witchcraft-generally ill-wishing or bewitching, alleged power to remove spells, which were sometimes a form of blackmail. Today witchcraft is not so common as it was, the scientists' wand is dissolving many things with the result that the old tales and legends are fading from the memories of the country folk. Witch-belief in its traditional form appears to have gone for ever.

It is natural, says a well-known authority on the subject, to think that magic is a thing of the past, which must have whithered to dust under the hard light of modern science and scepticism, but this he maintains is not the case. Magical thinking is still deeply embedded in the human mentality and even today it attracts interest and support.

There is certainly a curious revival of interest in witchcraft, black magic and the like, probably because things occult are so widely discussed nowadays. Though witchcraft and black magic do not touch the finner issue of the occult. Cornish wise men and women, once got a good living out of practising their so-called witchcraft. They could be consulted for casting and removing spells and curses. One famous Cornish wizard, as he called himself, attended the Law Courts at Bodmin, and undertook to keep witchcraft off farms for a shilling a year and in addition guarantee no further trouble.

Another could not only remove spells cast on man and beast, but could look into the future and predict things to come with uncanny accuracy. Others again could charm snakes, and moles, stop or staunch the flow of blood, charm burns and scalds, take away ringworms and vermin and even find water and buried treasure.

Their sometimes roguish skill they pitted against the simple countryman and woman, " but after all " said a Cornish farmer to me, " who could resist the lifting of a spell from cattle or milk for a few shillings."

The ailments of animals and their care are important to farming folk and the help of a charmer or even a gypsy is well worth the trouble.

In my search I discovered there were men and women in our Cornish villages and moorland areas who believed in witches and the power of the evil eye as well as in the fairy folk.

They were known as the "Devil's" agents, and consisted of black, grey, and white. The black variety were believed to have unlimited power of doing evil and were usually malicious, cunning theives, and afflectors of children, cattle and crops. The grey witches were a mixture of good and bad ; they could cast a spell on one hand, and for a further consideration, remove it with the other, while the white

36

variety the " dogooders," were known in Cornwall as Pellars, they had the power to help but not to harm. The magic they used was for healing the sick or curing disease and various ailments, through the medium of charms.

It is curious to observe how many of the beliefs of our fathers and fore-fathers thrown aside long ago as mere old wives' tales reappear as real and well attested phenomena.

The miraculous cures and equally miraculous curses, which were believed to have been the effect of words, charms, spells, or incantations, in which—and here lies the secret of their power—the person affected had implicit belief.

It has seemed absurd to our modern minds that the mere recitation of a sentence, or even a meaningless jargon of words, or the wearing of a charm, should be able to cause such material results as the cure of apparent paralysis, the complete removal of warts, the production of skin eruptions, fits, the symptoms of definite disease, and even death, but with the new light which the study of psychology has thrown upon the working of the nervous centres such occurrences are not only well attested but scientifically explained.

It is, indeed, now an accepted scientific fact that the effect of the action of the brain on the material substance of the body is most powerful.

The real secret of witch-belief lies in the nature of the mind itself and the whole problem of what pyschologists call projection.

Although the so-called black witches are not now so common in Cornwall, like Devon we still have our folk medicine, which includes charms, incantations, and the traditional habits and customs relative to the preservation of health and the cure of disease. It is amazing that there are still a large number of people who hold in great reverence many herbs which they use to cure divers diseases, often accompanying their application even as did the Druids with sundry mystical charms.

These charms are held in high estimation and are carefully handed down from one generation to another ; there are some families in Cornwall who have been charmers for generations, thus they are preserved to their full efficiency.

Here again in seeking out, I have experienced great difficulty in obtaining the words of many of the charms used for the efficacy as many of them are destroyed as soon as they are told or recorded in print.

Yes, there are still people who can successfully charm warts and burns and scalds, stop the flow of blood, charm various complaints of the eyes, relieve and cure various skin complaints, charm snake bites and even charm snakes themselves. I have actually seen a snake charmed, have witnessed the stopping of blood from a badly cut and bleeding wrist, and been present when an old lady successfully charmed a badly scalded leg.

In a recent talk on Cornish Charms and Charmers to the members of a Cornish Young Farmers' Club, no less than five young farmers told me their respective fathers or grandfathers could charm ringworms in humans and cattle and it was not always necessary for the cattle or the patient to be seen by the charmer, they could be charmed over the telephone. The same applied to the charming of warts, and in the case of burns and scalds sometimes the charmer saw the sufferer, in others all that was required was a garment or some possession of the sufferer. This was charmed, returned to the patient, and placed on the burn or scald.

Quite recently I was intrigued to see a number of black slugs impaled on a thorn tree in a cottage garden. Enquiries revealed it was a cure for warts.

" Get" said the charmer, " a black slug and slit it open to show the white inside, and rub this over the wart, then pin the still live slug to a thorn tree during the new moon, or the waning of the moon, which ever happens to be. As the slug dried up the wart will fall off and be gone by the full moon."

The belief that warts can be charmed by sending the number to a charmer was illustrated to me when I was shown a postcard to the wart charmer which read, " I have 18 warts on my hand. Yours obediently."

" Let us laugh at the folly of our forefathers by all means," was a remark made to me by a person who had been successfully charmed, " but it does not therefore follow that our means to an end are more efficious though being presumably more sensible."

Strange and cuious things still happen in the country and as a Devonshire writer on Folklore says the outstanding point about black witchcraft lies not in its practice, but in the lingering belief that it can still operate. Much has been written of late on the subject of the black arts and of alleged existence and practice in the westcountry, but as far as I am concerned, I have found no evidence of this. The supposed witchcraft signs and symbols I have inspected in churchyards and desolate and direlict buildings have never been authentic, just rubbishly scribblings and oddments as pranks and jokes by young people out for kicks.

The following is an example. Quite recently a university student came with her friend to see me to say she had been threatened with dreadful happenings if she did not join a Black Magic session. So persistent was the dabber in these diabolical practices that he handed the young woman a piece of paper on which was written sundry mystical signs and told her that if she did not join the session on her return to college dire consequences would follow.

The young woman was naturally upset but I was able to assure her that the supposed curse on her piece of paper was complete rubbish, and the person who had written it and indeed, threatened her, was a swindler of the first order who was attempting to practice the most contemptible form of deception.

To laugh at the folly of witchcraft is the only way of being influenced by it, is the advice I offer.

TALES OF CORNISH WITCHES.

By WILLIAM H. PAYNTER (Recorder, Callington Old
Cornwall Society).

FEW Cornish people, probably, are aware how widespread
was the belief only a few years ago in charms and
charmers, and all other superstitions; or that there were
witches in almost every village, shunned and dreaded by
some, who feared their supposed power to ill wish those who
offended them, and sought out by others, who wanted by
their aid to avert the evil eye, or by their magic to remove
spells already cast on them or their cattle by an ill wisher
who had overlooked them.

The following is a selection from the many witch tales
I have collected during the past six months in various parts
of the Duchy.

THE BEWITCHED Cow.—A farmer living not far from
Launceston had a cow which was suddenly taken ill with a
mysterious sickness. A cow-doctor was sent for, but was
unable to do anything for the suffering animal. At length
the farmer was advised to visit an old man in the district
who was known to be well versed in witchcraft. He did so,
when on payment of certain fees the witch visited
the farm, and after inspecting the animal came to
the conclusion that it was bewitched. "Well," said the
farmer, "what can I do about it?" "I'll tell you,

replied the wise man; "take a handful of salt, and go at sunrise to the cowhouse and sprinkle it about the building. Cast what remains over the door of the house, turning east while you are so doing, but be very careful with the salt; on no account let any of it fall into the hands of your enemy (meaning the person who had ill-wished him), for with it a lot more harm could be done." The farmer did as directed, and within a few days the cow was in perfect health again.

WHOLE FARM BEWITCHED.—A large farm in the Tintagel district was some years ago bewitched on an extensive scale. Everything went wrong; day after day the cattle died; the cows would give no milk; the crops were a failure, and even the butter would not turn. Hearing of a celebrated "White Witch,' residing at Plymouth, the farmer and his wife undertook the journey to seek his aid. The witch, it appears, was a man of wonderful gifts, and showed a most uncanny knowledge of the farmer's affairs before any information was imparted to him. This so impressed the farmer that he at once engaged him to visit his farm and remove the evil spell. The witch duly arrived, and after great preparations ordered all the household, including the farm hands, to prepare themselves wi h lighted candles and lanterns. At midnight they all assembled and comn enced to perambulate the farm; every field, stable, linhay and house was visited—the witch walking in front "saying words" and reading something out of a book with the result that the evil spell was removed and the cattle and crops again flourished. This reminds one of the medieval way of exorcising, by the priest, with bell, book, and candle; but as far as I can gather no bell was used in this curious ceremony.

A DELABOLE WITCH.—A neighbour of mine, said a lady near Tintagel, once had an attack of what is locally called "wildfire" (meaning shingles). For days she suffered much pain, and was at last advised to visit "Old Ann," the witch of Delabole. Being unable to undertake the journey, she sent an aunt, who took with her three handkerchiefs. One of these Ann charmed by putting her hand on it and uttering an incantation. She then commenced the homeward journey, just over five miles, and on arriving placed the handkerchief on the affected part; but the curious thing was, the sufferer was already better before she arrived, for she began to improve at the very time the spell was laid, though she had no idea of the hour her aunt was going to the witch.

This old dame, I find, was consulted by many people in the Delabole district, including an old woman living at Trewarmett, who suffered from a sore leg. The same method was employed, namely the charmed handkerchief. In the directions given, the handkerchief had to be placed on the affected spot from above downwards, that is, striking it towards the toes ; the evil would then ooze out from the feet instead of being driven higher up the body.

Two Callington Farmers Bewitched.— During a recent lecture at Callington the following stories were related to me, showing how two local farmers were bewitched, and how the spells were successfully removed after a visit to the great White Witch at Plymouth. In the first case the farmer, who had his farm stock ill-wished, was ordered to take the heart of one of the animals which had met with a mysterious death, stick it full of pins and needles, and burn it in the centre of one of his fields at midnight, at the same time uttering some strange words which the white witch enunciated. This he did, and the spell was immediately removed. In the second instance the witch produced in some mysterious way the photograph of the ill-wisher, and the farmer was requested to strike the unfortunate woman whom it happened to portray on any part of her body, but not with intent to kill. He struck the portrait, as requested, across the leg, and was told after paying the usual fee that on his homeward journey he would find her lying by the roadside with her leg broken. Sure enough, he did, just outside the town, and the spell was at once removed, or at least it was said he suffered no further losses !

The Ill-wished Cows.—A farmer of Saint Mellion had three dairy-cows to let, and an old woman, who was known as a witch, living near, offered to take them. As the farmer did not like her, he would not make a bargain with her, but agreed with another neighbour for the dairy. When the woman heard who had been preferred, she informed everyone she met that old " so-and-so," the man who had taken the cows, should rue the day that he ventured to cross her path.

"I will lay such a spell," said she, "that he will wish he had never seen the cows." After a few days, the new owner and his wife came to the farmer one night and said how they believed the cows must be ill-wished, for the milk daily went to curds. The farmer was greatly puzzled when he heard this news, for it was early spring ; however, he exchanged them for three others, but, alas, the milk of these also "runned." Things then began to go wrong with him and his family, till at last he was obliged to take back his cows because they had, as he stated, "no profit in them." Meanwhile the old witch who had coveted them bragged how she had served him, and stated how she had been on her knees under a white-thorn tree growing by the cross-roads ; and there, for the best part of the night, had called on " the powers " till they had helped her to cast the spell that had turned the cows' milk into junket (One is tempted to wonder why this witch, who was very proud to be known as such, chose the cross-road thorn as a suitable place for her evil work. Was it because such trees were said to have sprung from stakes driven into suicides graves ?).

A HELSTON WITCH. — About seventy years ago, a woman living near Helston had a child affected with a mysterious sickness, to cure which medical aid had been in vain tried. As it was generally believed in the neighbourhood that the child was " ill-wished " the woman was advised to go into Helston and see Tamson Blight, the witch, who it was said had the power of discovering who had bewitched it, and of compelling them to remove their influence. A visit was accoidingly made, and the woman demanded of Tamson the name of the ill-wisher. This she refused to give, but she described the ill-wisher in such clear detail that the woman immediately named the sorcerer, and returned home resolved to "bring blood from her." Some days afterwards the reputed witch passed her door, so she laid violent hands upon her and scratched her arm, drawing blood. Strange to relate, from that hour the child began to get well, and was soon able to leave her bed and play with the other children, free from all disease.

Here, again, it is interesting to note that the drawing of a witch's blood was mentioned in the twelfth century by Glanvil, who relates that when Jane Brooks, known as the " demon of Tedworth," bewitched a boy, his father scratched her face and drew blood, whereupon the boy instantly exclaimed that he was well. Shakespeare also alludes to the same practice in "Henry VI.," Pt. I., Act I., sc. v., where Lord Talbot says to Joan of Arc, " Blood will I draw on thee, thou art a witch." A man living at Camborne recently informed me that he met a woman who knew Tamson Blight, or " Tammy Blee " as she was more commonly known, quite well ; in fact her husba.id when a child used to be put to bed with her, while his mother went about her business. He relates that before she died she was confined to her bed for a considerable time. Often people were brought on stretchers and laid at her bedside entirely help-less, and they were known to rise up and go down over the stairs perfectly well.

THE COCK, THE FARMER AND THE BRANDIS.—The following was related to me by an old lady over eighty years of age, who knew, and was even well acquainted with, a witch in the Helston district. " When I was a girl," said the old dame, " my master suffered many losses, which he attributed to the malign influences of some evil-disposed person. The help of the witch was sought, and she advised as follows, " Go home, catch the cock, put him under the brandis (an iron tripod, in common use with fires on the hearth for supporting crock or kettle) and cover him over with a red cloth. Then call together all your friends and neighbours and give them plenty to eat, and before their departure let each one stroke the brandis, and the cock will crow over the one who stole." Returning home, the farmer did as directed, and each one in turn was requested to go through the ordeal. Now it happened that one old woman present refused, but the farmer, not wishing to be outdone, forced her. Immediately she neared the brandis the cock crew, and she thereupon made a confession, in which she stared that she alone was responsible for the ill-luck he had had.

THE WIZARD OF THE WEST. — While discussing the mysterious fraternity of wizards and witches with an old man well over eighty, he informed me that about forty-five years ago he attended the Assizes at Bodmin, and after the necessary business had been got through a dinner was held, at which all the chief of the county were assembled, including many prominent farmers. Just before the dinner was timed to commence a strange individual, dressed in a long white shirt, entered the room. He was at once hailed by the farmers present as the "Wizard of the West," and each in turn paid him a sum of money to keep "witchcraft" off their farms during the ensuing twelve months. Later in the evening, says my informant, the wizard was discovered drunk, and certain members, who during the year had been "over-looked" or "ill-wished" in spite of having bought his protection, tried to set alight to his shirt, but he escaped, and was not seen again until the following year, when he once more appeared to collect his dues.

CORNISH CUNNING FOLK

During the 19th Century, the activities of Cornish cunning folk received widespread attention both from the press and the judiciary. The most famous and well documented cunning folk were Tamsin or Thomasine Blight and her husband, Jimmy or James Thomas (otherwise known as Chegwin). So memorable were they among the Cornish that even William Lovett, the famous political activist, recalled: " Anything that Aunt Tammy took a fancy to, few who feared her dared to refuse..."("Life And Struggles Of William Lovett (192) Vol. 1, p.18)) And such was Tammy's fame that, in her later years, her portrait was painted by a leading artist of the day.

But apart from Tammy, there were a number of other practitioners who enjoyed a considerable reputation as cunning folk between Falmouth and Lands End. Some were referred to as "white witches", others as "wizards" or even "conjurors." These terms were often quite interchangeable, although historians have often maintained that they described very different roles. Another category, however, that of the charmer, seems to have been truly distinct. Several commentators of the period (including the folklorist Margaret Courtney of Penzance) believed that the talents of the "white witch" were inherited by a daughter from her father or a son from his mother - and this was a widespread belief.

Another term peculiar to the tradition of the white witch was the pellar (also spelt peller), although the latter spelling was less common.) The word appears to be a contraction of "repeller", meaning one who could repel a spell or an ill wish. Again, the term was often interchangeable with "white witch" and was not restricted in terms of gender. In the 20th century, of course, the terms of "black" and "white " witch are no longer acceptable to neo-pagans, but this was certainly not the case in 19th century Britain. Tamsin Blight is often referred to by William Bottrell, the greatest of folk tale compilers as a "pellar" and also "witch." Margaret Courtney claimed that there was a distinction between pellar and white witch and that the white witch did not have "powers... as great as those of a pellar, but they were thoroughly believed in; and consulted on every occasion for every complaint." (Cornish Feasts & Folklore). According to folk belief, the most noted pellars could be the seventh son of a seventh son or the seventh daughter of a seventh daughter. However, anyone who touched the famous Logan rock near Lands End could become a white witch. It is clear from Courtney's account of a white witch whom she knew (who was also a knitser) that she conformed to the pattern of activity and reputation of most West Country cunning folk for the woman in question could "cure people sitting by her fireside if they were miles away." She was also "consulted about the recovery of stolen property which, by casting (her) spells over the thief, it is still supposed (she) can compel him to return." The unnamed woman, whom she had known for 12 years, was regarded with awe by Margaret Courtney's maids, "who lived in great fear of her "ill wishing" them."

Confusingly, William Bottrell uses the terms "white witch" and "charmer" synonymously. When describing a woman known to him who lived in a hut in the hamlet of Treen (near Zennor), the woman had "charms for all kinds of skin diseases, salves for wounds and bruises, water of her own distilling for tender eyes..." However, she was also able to "put a spell of pain on anyone (though unknown to her) who illwished, begrudged or overlooked... any person or anything... She also knew enough of the black art to become a witch if she had a mind to..."

It was the folklorist Robert Hunt (Popular Romances Of The West Of England, 1871) who established the idea of Cornish witches gathering at the midsummer in the village of Trava - a
tradition among witches which is certainly quite rare, even in folklore, let alone history. He repeats the assertion found elsewhere by late 19th Century commentators that one could become a witch by getting onto the Giant's Rock or Logan Stone at Zennor "nine times without shaking it." This legend appears nowhere in the folk annals of Cornwall and I incline to the view that it is probably Hunt's own invention, probably based on Continental beliefs about witchcraft. Bottrell's own view about the collective activities of witches relates to the St Levan witches who, he believes "in days of yore (were) much addicted to the practice of necromancy, particularly witchcraft." He goes on to say that they held their revels at Castle Trereen (Treryn Dinas) and that they flew on ragwort stalks to Wales, Brittany and Spain. The Tol-pedn (Penwith) was apparently her place of assembly. It is possible that Bottrell, a St Levan man, may have inherited this view from older members of his family, in which case we can say with some certainty that the belief probably dates back to the 18th Century.

Whatever the folk beliefs shared by the Cornish at the time when Bottrell and Hunt were collecting their tales, the reality was that the fear of witches and

*Childbirth was very
dangerous for women
before modern medicine,
with one in eight first-time
mothers dying in labour, so
magic charms were
routinely used to protect
women.*

their power to work maleficium was uppermost in the minds of the populace. This in itself accounts for the widespread support for the cunning folk or pellars.

One commentator who carefully chronicled the superstitions of his local community at Polperro during the mid to late 19th century was Doctor Thomas Quiller-Couch. During the 1860's he published a number of papers in the Journal Of The Penzance Antiquarian & Natural History Society relating to cunning folk. According to Quiller-Couch, who collected mainly in the south eastern part of Cornwall:

"When witchcraft is suspected, the person "overlooked" has immediate recourse to the conjuror, the very bad representation of the astrologer of a former age. The conjuror is an important character in a Cornish village. He is resorted to by despairing lovers: he counsels those under the evil eye, and discloses the whereabouts of stolen goods. His answers, too, are given with true oracular ambiguity. "Our horn eat own corn" was his reply to a person who consulted him about the disappearance of various little household articles when appealed to in cases of suspected witchcraft, the certainty of weird influence is proved beyond doubt, and the first letter of the witch's name, or a description of her person, is given, or even, it is said, her bodily presence depicted on a mirror." (Couch: Antiquities of Polperro & Its Neighbourhood, paper 2)

Interestingly, Couch goes on to distinguish between the activities thus described, the province of the white witch and the charmer, whom he describes as "generally an elderly female, supposed to be gifted with supernatural power, which she exercises for good. By her own incantations and ceremonies she stops blood, and cures inflamed eyes and erysipelas."

Through the pages of the newspapers of the period we can find extensive references to the activities and careers of the white witches, conjurors and charmers of the 19th Century. One of the earliest references dates from 1824. (West Briton, 25th June 1824). A man named French who lived in Davidstow (3 miles from Camelford, North Cornwall) owned a team of horses but three of the four died suddenly. He purchased two new horses but these also died. Desperate, he travelled to Devon where he consulted a "celebrated wizard." The wizard provided him with a description of the suspected witch and he was advised to return to Camelford and seek her out. Subsequently he sold his hay to a clergyman and it was found to be laced with arsenic. The story is an interesting one because it suggests to us that people like French would travel miles to obtain a consultation and that their solutions were not necessarily accurate.

By the 1820's Tamsin or Thomasine Blight had established herself as a cunning woman of considerable power and influence in the Redruth area. Born in 1798, she had spent her early years working as a "bal maiden" in the Redruth/Illogan area. In 1835 she was to marry James Chegwin (alias Jemmy Thomas), a man of dubious credentials with whom she carried on an uneven alliance for many years until she removed herself to Breage (near Helston) and semi-retirement. In 1825 a woman afflicted with scrofula (or "The King's Evil") set out from St Ives in a carriage one Sunday morning to obtain the benefit of Tamsin's advice. With her in the carriage were two female neighbours and a child (West Briton, 26 Aug 1825). In those days there was no bridge between Hayle and St Ives. When they got half way across the estuary the driver of the carriage decided that the woman would benefit more from a dip than a charm and he then "brutally threw the patient and one of her companions into a stream which crosses the sands."

Twelve years after the consultation with the Devon witch, we find another reference to a farmer from St Ewe (WB: 28 Oct. 1836) whose child suffered from an eye disease. The mother of the child, whilst in Plymouth, was advised by a friend that she should consult a white witch in order to "expel the influence of the black witch" or "the child would never recover..." The mother paid for the cunning woman's transport and on arriving, was able to advise her as to the author of the child's illness.

Seven years later the West Briton was again seized with sensation (WB 3 Dec. 1841) when reporting a case of "Witchery Near Tywardreath". Apparently a village near Tywardreath had been plagued by a woman who had been suspected of causing several people's deaths through her incantations. One person, who had been ill for a while, had heard of a witchfinder (also referred to as a wise man) who lived at Mevagissey. Since he was visiting a nearby village, he intervened and "pronounced the case to be one of decided witchcraft." And here we are given a tantalising glimpse into the inititation of a witch for we are told that she took the sacrament and, when drinking the wine, repeated "the Lord's prayer thrice backwards...

securing the bread and giving it to a toad." We are not told whether the toad was a familiar but it is highly likely that it was since the principle of animal familiars such as mice or toads was very common.

One of the functions of the white witch or pellar was that of retrieving stolen property and, in this regard, Tamsin Blight and her husband Jemmy enjoyed considerable success. In small rural communities this facility was not quite as difficult as it might be today for local knowledge was something very easily obtained by the pellar and used to his or her advantage. However, in 1841, when Tamsin was already in her 40's, the Penzance Gazette reported an intriguing case involving the theft of a mahogany work box, containing cash and other valuables (Wed. Sept. 22, 1841). The box had been stolen from the apartment of a Mr Sam Morris, the driver of the Falmouth and Penzance coach. The following morning, Morris' wife travelled to Redruth to visit the "conjuror" and was informed that the money would be restored "not all at once, but at three different times: that before her return all the gold except one sovereign... would be thrown in at the door, and that the box would also be returned uninjured."

When Mrs Morris returned to Falmouth, her neighbours informed her that some one had thrown several sovereigns and half sovereigns into the passage of the house. On counting the money, she found it one sovereign short. However, on the following evening a woman wearing a shawl over her head stopped two boys some way from the house and gave them a parcel, instructing them to take it to Mrs Morris. The parcel, on being opened, contained the rest of the money and a letter explaining that the box would be found on the steps of a house on the back hill.

So successful was the conclusion to this case that according to the reporter, it "re-established the wavering faith of many persons in witchcraft." In fact this was not the first or indeed the last example of Tamsin's uncanny ability to restore stolen goods to their rightful owner. The year before (14 Feb. 1840), the West Briton had reported a theft of 30 sovereigns from a Joseph Jewell of Praze, near Crowan. In this case, Jewell spread the rumour that he would be consulting "the conjuror" and the bag with 20 sovereigns then turned up in a hayrick a few days later. Such was the reputation enjoyed by Tamsin, it seems, that the criminal decided to cut his losses.

One of the most amusing and dramatic stories about Tamsin and Jemmy concerns a ritual necromantic summoning of the spirit of a woman in Stithians churchyard (near Helston) in order to locate the deceased's will and effects. During the ritual, Tamsin's client discovers that the spirit is in fact Jemmy after all. The incident may possibly have been based on a real exploit. According to the West Briton (6 Sept. 1844), the churchyard at Phillack (near Hayle) was "made the scene of transactions which would have blackened the darkest ignorance of bygone ages." A "scatterer of witch spells from Helston" was then engaged and, after payment was made, "the spell breaker commenced the mysteries of his art, by making mysterious sounds and performing mysterious actions, as he walked over the dead, hotly pressed by his frightened dupes." After he (i.e. Jemmy) had walked round the church several times, "the persons who had ill-wished (his clients) were brought to their face. Thus the spell was dissolved."

Here we have the germ of the story later recorded by Bottrell. The latter has simply altered the location and the modus operandi.

In May 1856, the editor of the West Briton had much to say about the activities of "gipsies, conjurors, fortune-tellers, and charmers... living now, in this nineteenth century, and artfully earning a livelihood out of the credulity of mankind. And, strange to tell, vast numbers of people love to have it so. If they are out of health, or lose animals by disease or accident, they straightway conclude that they are bewitched and away they go to the professional conjuror." The article goes on to comment that "It used to be Johnny Hooper, of Ladock; it is now Mr....Thomas, of Nanstallan, in the parish of Bodmin. (This is in fact John Thomas. He later moved to Illogan.) This man carried on a flourishing trade in the conjuring way, and seldom goes home from a fair or market quite sober, and withal is an immoderate snuff taker."

In 1856 Tamsin, who had been estranged from Jemmy for some years and had been living in a small cottage near to Breage church, died. Jemmy was to live on for another 18 years and was once again mentioned as a "wizard", still resident in Helston. On 24th August 1866, we find this reference to him:

"Within 20 miles of Buryan (a village between Penzance and Lands End), there lives a veritable "white witch", who practises divinations and sorceries and detects thefts and murders... That the fame of this "white witch" is probably spread from one end of Cornwall to the other is tolerably well established. A few days since the sergeant of police in Penzance met in one

53

of the streets of that town, at three o'clock in the morning, exposed to a pitiless rain, and drenched to the skin, an old woman of sixty, and her daughter of about twenty. The latter had a babe in her arms."

The threesome had apparently been burgled. Finding the Buryan policeman out, they set out on foot for Helston (20 miles away) but, finding the wizard not at home, they had to return, only to begin their journey once more." The tenacity of the threesome and their utter conviction that they could recover the goods is very much in evidence here.

On the 26th of February 1874, the West Briton announced the demise of the former pellar of Bodmin, John Thomas. Not much is known about him today, but, according to the obituary that appeared about him, "Rich and poor for miles around... honoured him with a visit (in times past)... Every species of ailment... he was supposed to cure ... Among horses he was indeed a host; a kicker might as well be a dead horse... after John had worked his will on him; and as to stopping blood, if an arm was lopped off, no blood would flow if John cried stop..."

Apart from Tamsin Blight and John Thomas, there were other, equally well known pellars thriving in Redruth and the Camborne area. An unnamed "wise woman" who lived near Camborne and who dispensed cures, attracted people to her front door from as far away as the Lizard Peninsula. It was said that when a leading specialist in Cornwall, Dr Montgomery, had announced a case to be hopeless, the sufferer was often taken to see the white witch. She was also reputed to have cured a woman of a haemorrhage. The woman was advised to drink warm beer and soon made a full recovery.

Uncle Jacky Hooper, mentioned by the West Briton in 1856, lived at Blowinghouse, near Redruth. His speciality was the cure of sick cattle which he healed by giving the owner a prayer or chapter from the Book of Proverbs to read over the animal's back (See Hamilton-Jenkin: Cornwall And Its People: 1932, p. 293). For this he charged 5 shillings - an expensive fee in those times. When he received visitors to his cottage, Hooper would light a lamp and smoke a piece of glass. He would then scry the glass to perceive the business on which the client had called.

One particular memory, recorded by Hamilton-Jenkin, regarding a woman called "Old Rose" (related to him by Mrs Stanley James), offers a vivid picture of the person and circumstances of the white witch:

"Clutching my father's hand, we knocked at the door of an old thatch - roofed apology for a house, entered in response to a thin, reedy voice piping "Come in," and stumbled our way across a nearly dark room, lit only by a tiny window, a foot square and mostly stuffed with rags. All sorts of dried herbs and mysterious things were hanging from the rafters overhead, but - most mysterious of all - away by an open fireplace, sitting on a stool, smoking a small pipe, was old Rose herself, looking in the shadows to be my childish ideal of a witch. What especially appealed to me was her claw-like hands..."

It is to the advantage of the historian that the Cornish pellars and "wizards" were often forced to appear at the local assizes for their exploits were then reported in the local newspapers. One practitioner who enjoyed notoriety on a par with Jimmy Thomas was William Rapson Oates, of Ludgvan. Described as a "herbalist and fortune teller, " he was arrested in July 1869 (WB, July 1869), at Bodmin Gaol, having just completed a nine month term of imprisonment (with hard labour) for robbing an elderly woman at Feock. On leaving prison, he visited a woman called Jane Trevena, described as a "quack doctress" in Redruth. He then borrowed £2. 5s. from her, saying his father would repay the money the following Wednesday and claiming to be a Mr Mayal, the son of the warder of Bodmin Gaol. It was said at his commital that he was "regularly engaged by farmers, both in Devon and Cornwall to keep away witchcraft from their cattle and doctor them."

By January 1894 (25 years later), he was still at it. This time he was at the assizes, accused of pretending to exercise witchcraft and sorcery. On December 29th Oates visited Mary Sedgman, where he told her her daughter was under a spell and he had the power to discover who had cast the spell. Claiming himself to be a certain Dr Thomas (a brother of the wizard Thomas of St Austell), he borrowed 3 shillings from Sedgman.

By September 1894 (WB, 10 Sept. 1894), we find him before the bench charged under the Vagrancy Act with being asleep on a seat in the Helston Bowling Green. "Being an old offender (he) was sent to prison for a fortnight."

55

When Couch collected his stories of Cornish witches and cunning folk in the district of Polperro, where he lived and worked, he included an account of two men whom he referred to as "astrologers", John Stevens and Harry Warne. Astrology, or fortune telling, as it was then commonly interpreted, had grown in popularity during the 19th Century and it was quite common for the cunning man or woman to include astrological predictions as part of their services to clients. Couch recalls the "astrologer" John Stevens, who died in 1849, aged 92, in some depth. By occupation, Stevens was a shoe maker, although of "studious habits". He employed his foretelling of his neighbours' fates for no fee or reward. However, he was unable to predict the date of his own demise.

Couch goes on to recall:

"After his death his library was found to consist of Ephemerides, and other books on the science of the stars and their government of human actions; some in quarto, and in black letter... In a round shallow box were found three plates of brass which, when combined, he called an orrery, having engraved on them representations of tables and diagrams of planetary motions. One of these plates was a dissected circle with astronomical signs and constellations, and a central hole, in which had been fixed a wire. By moving this over the area he traced the conjunction of the planets, and so resolved the horoscope of the person consulting. His daughter stated that within her knowledge, this instrument had cost him in repairs twenty four shillings, which was a large sum to a man in his station of life."

If east Cornwall had its "astrologers", then West Cornwall appeared to have the highest population of "wizards" and charmers. According to the Reverend Joseph Hammond, writing in 1897, ("Our Cornish Parish: London: Skeffington & Sons, 1897), Redruth "would seem to be rich" in them. He mentions several names (although anonymously).

"For over 20 years B- M- has driven a lucrative trade as a fortune teller... Those who have satisfied her modest demands learn that they will marry well, then go abroad to amass wealth, with which they will return to live happily ever afterwards."

The fame of this fortune teller had apparently spread to London. There was also a Mrs G., a wise woman who charged "three and a tanner", or accepted payment in kind. There was, in addition to these illustrious ladies, a A- R-, who charmed blood, M.E., who owned a kennel stone and who cured eye complaints (a kennel was an eye disease), J.P. who was renowned for his poultices and Jimmy the wizard of Camborne who was proficient in all aspects of his craft.

As can be seen from these accounts in the 19th century, the Cornish not only believed profoundly in the effects of ill wishing but made full opportunity of consulting the pellars, charmers and cunning folk for the purposes of divination, healing and the recovery of stolen property. And when such folk did not live in their immediate vicinity, they were prepared to travel immense distances to engage their services. They enjoyed high esteem among the working classes of the time and were highly successful operators of the occult.

Witchcraft in Cornwall.—At the monthly meeting of the
Penzance Natural History and Antiquarian Society, held February
3rd, 1882, the chairman, Mr. W. C. Borlase, M.P., said he had
brought a curious old tract entitled " A true account of a strange and
wonderful relation of one John Tonken, of Pensans, in Cornwall, said
to be bewitched by some women, two of whom on suspicion are committed to prison ; he vomitted up several pins, pieces of walnut-shells,
an ear of rye with a straw half-a-yard long, and rushes of the same
length, all of which are kept to be shown at the next assizes for the
said county. This may be printed, R. P. London. Printed by
George Croom, at the Blue Ball in Thames Street, near Baynard's
Castle, 1686." The account went on to say that " John Tonken, of
Pensans, near the Mount in Cornwall," who was 15 or 16 years of

age, was " in April last strangely taken with sudden fits," and that on May 4th, 1686, as he was in bed, there appeared to him " a woman in a blue jerkin and red petticoat, with yellow and green patches," who told him he would not be well until he brought up the above-mentioned articles. Two old women were taken up on suspicion of having bewitched him ; and the story ended by the expression of a hope that if the women were guilty they would be found out at the next assize " and so receive the reward due to their merits; " the names of Peter Jenkin, mayor, and John Jose (which should be Grose) justice, being subscribed to the tract. That tract took them back to one of the most horrible times in English history. One of the things most deeply to be deplored in Puritanism was that the texts of the Bible were taken so literally that some of these texts offered to zealous and fanatical people grounds for behaving in a most cruel manner, and, among other things, the persecution of witches was the most prominent. He did not believe the general opinion was that this fanaticism extended very much into Cornwall. It would be extremely interesting to know what had been the end of the two poor old women. There was a picture attached to the tract of Matthew Hopkins, the witch-hunter, one of the most execrable scoundrels in English history, for it was to his evidence that a great many of these poor people owed the shocking and abominable death, preceded by torture, which they suffered.

xxviii. *Superstition in Cornwall.*—At a meeting of the same society on 10th March, 1882, the Rev. S. Rundle, vicar of Godolphin, read a very interesting paper on " Cornish superstitions." There could be no doubt, he said, that belief in charms and ghosts—the two most popular forms of Cornish superstition—was by no means on the wane. People may be a little more chary of expressing their convictions on the subject, yet all kinds of persons down in their heart retained a very strong opinion that ghosts still walked, that witches can still charm, and that persons can still be ill-wished. A farmer, for instance, would refuse to take some parochial office, because in the discharge of its duties he was likely to offend some woman that had the power of ill-wishing his cows. People, however, whilst openly confessing their belief in charms, would not talk about ghosts till they were quite sure they would not be laughed at. To begin with charms : it had been stated there may be a great deal said in favour of actual good being done by them because they generally ended with an invocation of the All-holy Trinity, thus showing a certain amount of faith. His experience, however, was that there was no such kind of faith displayed : they said " If you could cure he, you can cure me." Members of a society like this should guard the ignorant against impostors, who swindled them out of their money by stating that they can take off the ill-wish. Two old women quarrelled separately about a flower-pot. One of them had a son, who was exceedingly ill. John Bostock, a famous white-witch of Exeter, happened to be on his periodical tour through Exeter, and he, declaring that the other old woman had bewitched the son, said for 11s. he would make some medicine that would make the curser's eyes fall out of her head. The 11s. was paid—though previously they could not have raised 1s.—and the medicine made. But the woman's eyes did not fall out, and the man was not cured. Inquiry was made after the impostor, but he managed to escape. An old woman once told him (the reader) she had been charming a kennel out of a baby's eye, and as he was of the opposite sex she could tell him the charm. It was to repeat " Two angels came, one with fire, one with water ; in water, out fire." The charm of the dead man's hand was very common. A woman suffering from a terrible tumour once told him she had walked two miles to lay a dead man's hand on it, but she was too late, for the coffin had been nailed down. Soon after her husband died ; it was his dying wish that after his death she should take his hand and place it upon the wound. However, she said he was too near to her, and therefore she could not do it. Shortly after a girl did use this charm, and supposed she was cured by it. The form was to take the hand, cross it nine times over the wound, and then, as the hand itself resolved itself into nothingness, so also would the wound disappear. A cure for sore throat was to take a piece of a birch broom and cross it nine times over the part affected. The woman who told him this assured him that she had been cured in this way. Once he was sent for to baptize a child, around whose neck hung a little bag which the mother said contained a bit of a donkey's ear, and that this charm had cured the child of a most distressing cough. Whenever a discharge of blood from the nostrils takes place a certain woman was told of it. Without leaving her house she was said to have such an influence upon the sufferer that the afflux ceased. She told him the charm consisted in saying a verse of the Psalms, but she could not read, and he was inclined to believe the form was, " Jesus came to the River Jordan and said, Stand and it stood, and so I bid thee blood stand in the name of the Father. the Son, and the Holy Ghost." Coming to ghosts, the author said certain sounds in mines were believed to be the old miners working underground ; and it was said that good luck had been met with in working in the direction of the knocking. Not long since a great many people on a Sunday afternoon assembled at a mine to hear the knocking, but after a time the " bucca" disappeared. Mr. Rundle next mentioned that about seven years ago he was staying in a Cornish country house. He knew nothing of the house, but he felt an indescribable awe whilst in the bedroom he occupied, although he heard no noises that he could not well account for. About nine months after his visit he was told that one of the servants who had lately come into the house fell down in a fit and by her screaming alarmed the whole household. After restoratives had been used she said she had seen an old gentleman wearing a wide-awake hat, a long cloak and list slippers, come out of the room in which he (Mr. Rundle) had felt a sense of awe, and cross to another ; and the girl's description was recognised as the exact description of an old gentleman who used to sleep in that room, and who was reported to have done exceedingly wicked things. The question he should like answered was, why did he feel that dreadful awe long before he knew anything of the ghost story. In his parish not long since a house was said to be haunted, and always having had a great fancy for solving such mysteries he resolved to pass a night in the house. Two persons in turn promised to share the adventure with him, but both failed; one said his wife would not like it, the

61

other was afraid of catching cold. A third man would have accompanied him, but before that the mystery was solved in this prosaic way. A couple had married upon a fortune so very private that no one knew where it was. The fortune notwithstanding, they got into debt, and were very anxious to return to their parents, who, however, refused to receive them, till one night the couple rushed to them saying their own house was haunted. In all such cases it would be wise to investigate and if possible to expose the falsehood. In conclusion, he ventured to disagree with the late Mr. Bottrell, who believed these legends were dying out. He believed legends were now in course of being formed. These beliefs in ghosts and charms would be only told to those for whom respect was felt.

The paper led to an interesting discussion.—Mrs. Ross remarked that education had resulted in developing a new form of the same belief—spiritualism. Some people could and some could not see ghosts. She was once staying with some friends in a house said to be haunted. She saw nor heard nothing, but her friends, who were by no means nervous or superstitious, believed they saw figures, and left, not because they were frightened, but it was annoying. People differed in the powers of the natural senses; why not in the powers of their supernatural senses? — Mr. Hosken Richards said a former servant of his wore a charm against fits.—Mrs. Ross mentioned that years ago it was believed a procession of coffins used to pass down Chapel Street, and it was reported that a woman who saw it said one of the coffins struck her, and she died the same night.—Mr. Uren thought the belief in ghosts, charms, and witchcraft would disappear only very slowly before the march of education. Some believed now that just before Christmas a coach with headless horses and coachmen drove from Tremough through the streets of Penryn, and that unless people turned their heads in a peculiar way they would be spirited away. At Trewarthenick, the seat of the Gregors, near Truro, the servants would not go in a certain part of the house after dark. Three or four years ago there was a haunted house at St. Just. Within very recent times a woman at Enys had a reputation for ill-wishing because the expressions of wishes in two cases (in one that a man would tumble off his horse and be killed, and in the other that a man's pigs would die and his cow wither) were literally fulfilled.— Mr. Marquand related that in Guernsey a family, formerly prosperous, had been ruined by the cattle being ill-wished.—Mr. Rundle mentioned that the cases he had given had all occurred within the last four years. He might also add that epileptic subjects had walked round the church at Godolphin at midnight and then stood before the altar. In one case a cure was said to be effected.—Miss Louise Courtney mentioned that at St. Just a young woman begged of young men as many pennies as would buy a silver ring, which was believed to be a cure for fits.—Mr. H. S. Hill related how he had seen a charm used for sore eyes, the lad's eyes being stroked with a silver ring said to have been taken from the hand of a man who was drowned; and mentioned that in Devonshire if a death occurred in a family the hives were put in mourning lest the bees should die.—Mr. Uren mentioned that he once saw thirty hives belonging to Mr. Joshua Fox, of Tregednex, tied up with crape because of a death in the Fox family; and the chairman, Mr. W. C. Borlase, said as a boy he remembered that when old Mrs. Botheras died at the "First and Last," Sennen, the birds'-cages and the flower-pots were tied up with crape to prevent the birds and plants dying. There was also the practice of going to the hives, knocking, and telling the bees of the death that had occurred.—Mr. Wildman said one of his earliest recollections was seeing a woman stroking a tumour in her neck with the hand of a man who had died on the edge of a limekiln in North Devon. And he related how he obtained a piece of rope a man was hanged with for a poor woman who had walked fourteen miles to Bodmin in the hope of getting it that she might effect the cure of her sore eyes. Within a few years the charm of the dead hand had been used in Penzance, and it was said efficaciously.

Charms

PERSONS who profess to work charms can be divided into three classes :—(1). The person who mutters a charm, offers a prayer and directs some herbal decoction to be taken. This comes very near faith-healing. (2). The ignorant person who has learnt a charm and mutters it on condition of receiving a gift of money. (3). The white witch or conjurer who professes to put spells on, or remove them from, persons or animals. A charm is transmitted orally and to the opposite sex.

CHARMS FOR KENNEL OR WHELK IN THE EYE :

(1) "Two angels came from the East. One brought fire, the other brought water:
In the name of the Father, Son and Holy Ghost."

(2) Boy must take a she-cat, and rub the cat's tail over his eye nine times.

CHARM FOR BURN : Blow on the place and say :—

"Two little angels came from the East. One brought fire, the other brought frost.
In the Name of the Father, Son and Holy Ghost."

CHARM FOR CORNS : You need not go to have them charmed.

Take off your shoe and stocking when you first see the new moon. Show your corn to the moon and say nine times : "Corns down heere ; Narry waun up theere."

CHARMS FOR CRICK :

(1) Person of opposite sex must walk over patient's back nine times.

(2) Person is drawn through a Men-an-tol nine times, against the sun.

CHARM FOR BLACKHEADS : Crawl nine times under a bramble which is rooted at both ends.

CHARM FOR STANCHING BLOOD : "Christ was born in Bethlehem, baptized in the river Jordan. There he digged a well and turned the water against the hill. So shall thy blood stand still. In the Name of the Father, Son and Holy Ghost."

HOOPING COUGH :

(1) Cut off some hair growing on the shoulder of a donkey (latter of opposite sex to sufferer), put it in a bag and wear it.

(2) Take a mouse, kill un, rooast un tell he's burnt to a cinder, beat un up as fine as powder, mix un in a basin of milk and give it to the cheeld to drink.

(3) Take some white bread, put it upon a white handkercher ; give the bread to a donkey ; taake the crumbs that fall 'pon the handkercher ; put them in milk, and give it to the cheeld.

FITS (Variation of one given by Miss Courtney) :

Beg 20 pennies, saying "Give me a penny." Buy a ring, paying the pennies across the counter in inverse order to • that in which they were received.

RHEUMATISM :

(1) Stand at the Church Door. Beg 30 pennies off worshippers without speaking. Change them for silver coin. Walk three times around the Communion Table saying the Gloria. The silver is made into a ring and worn by the sufferer.

(2) Carry a potato in your pocket.

TOOTHACHE :

(1) Go to door of Church. Put finger on fifth nail from latch or keyhole and say Creed three times.

(2) Put on left stocking first every morning.

(3) Bite a tooth from a skull and carry it in your pocket.

C. C. JAMES.

An Old Remedy

From the *Gentleman's Magazine,* 1735

———

Lamorran, Cornwall,
Sept. 26, 1735.

" Mr. Urban,

In your Magazine for August last, you have obliged the Publick with Dr. Mead's Receipt for the Bite of a Mad Dog ; no doubt it is a very good one, because attested by the Experience of so ingenious and learned a Physician. Tho' I am no Professor of that Science, I shall presume to send you one that I have experienced for several years, and on a vast Number of the Irrational Kind, viz., Bullocks, Horses, Dogs, etc., without ever once failing ; and is as followeth.

Take Primrose Roots, Star of the Earth, dry Mouse Ear, and green Mouse Ear, of each a handful, cut small and well boil'd in a Quart of Milk ; add the black of one Crab's Claw finely powder'd, sweeten it well with Venice or London Treacle. A Drench for one Dog, etc., to be repeated three Mornings successively fasting, the sooner the better, for after the Creature is once Mad, I believe there is no cure.

Quaere, whether proper for human Constitutions, if so, 'tis not quite so troublesome to comply with, as with the Doctor's. But this I shall leave to better Judgments, having never tried it on any rational Creature.

Star of the Earth is generally found on old dry clay Ground, that has been seldom or never Plough'd ; Mouse Ear, is an Herb that sometimes resembles the form of a Mouse's Ear, and is hairy on one side."

B.S.

CURIOUS EAST CORNWALL CURES.

The following remarkable recipes, which have been given to me as cures for the thrush and whooping-cough, illustrate the widespread belief in superstitions that existed in East Cornwall only a few years ago. A cure for the thrush (a disease of the mouth and throat):—Procure six threads of cotton, pass them separately through a cat's mouth, and then through the mouth of the sufferer; after so doing, throw the threads into a stream, and as the current bears them away, so will the complaint disappear. Now three cures for whooping-cough:—Cut two hairs from the shoulder of a donkey, put them in a little bag and fasten the bag around the child's neck.—Gather nine spar-stones from a stream that divides two parishes, taking care not to interrupt the free passage of the water in so doing. Then dip a quart of water from the stream, which must be taken in the direction in which the stream runs; by no means must the vessels be dipped against the stream. Then make the nine stones red-hot, and throw them into the quart of water. Bottle this prepared water, and give the affected child a wine-glass of it for nine mornings following, and the cough will entirely disappear.

Take a hair from the patient's head and place it between slices of bread-and-butter and give it to a dog to eat, if he (the dog) in eating it coughs, then will the whooping-cough be transferred to it, and the child will get well.

W. H. PAYNTER

RATTLE-BONES AND PANCAKES.

The observance in connectson with Shrove Tuesday or Pancake Day, began at Callington (about 30 years ago) on

the day preceding, which was termed "Rattlebone Night."
As soon as it became dusk the boys of the town appeared
with numerous empty tins and buckets, which, after being
securely tied together, were drawn through the streets accompanied by much shouting and the chanting of the
following :—

> "Rattlebones, Rattlebones,
> Give us some pancake and we'll be gone ;
> But if you give us none,
> We'll throw a stone,
> And down your door shall come."

From what I can gather the boys were supposed to represent
the imps of darkness, that seized on and exposed all that was
unguarded.

It is also interesting to note that Shrove Tuesday was
considered by the farmers in East Cornwall as a holiday, or
at least a ceasing of very heavy work on the land, and
everyone in their employ joined in the pancake-feast. One
and all assembled round the fire, and each had to toss a cake
before he had it for his supper. The awkwardness of some
of the tossers, who were compelled to eat their share, even if
it fell into the ashes, afforded great amusement.

————
W. H. PAYNTER.

KING'S EVIL.

About twenty years ago, said my informant, a man living
near Callington suffered from swellings in the neck and
shoulder, which were thought to be King's Evil. Various
remedies were tried, but without success. At last he was
was advised to visit a local White Witch, who was noted
for curing complaints by the touch of a hangman's rope.
He accordingly went, and described how the witch first
muttered some strange words and then stroked the affected
part with a piece of rope, with which he said a man had
been hanged, and strange to say, within a short space of
time, the disease completely disappeared.

Knowing the son of this old man, I made a number of
enquiries, and discovered that the valuable relic, had been in
the possession of the family for a great number of years,
and was secured at Launceston after a public execution.

It was not difficult of course to procure such rope in the
good old days, when sheep-stealers, and even others guilty
of less offences, were publicly hanged.

W. H. Paynter.

Mrs. Rosewarne's grandfather would row down from St. Ives to the Wolf Rock in his small boat (The *Threeha'pard*) to catch hake; and would often remark to his wife, "No wonder they call it the Wolf, 'Becca, for the roaring of the sea, round the rock and under it, is awful—exactly like wolves howling."

This old man, Mr. Perkin, owned two boats which were named *Threeha'pard* and *Twopennard*.

During the Napoleonic Wars, when scares of a French landing were frequent, he would comfort his grandchildren by saying, "Never mind my dears, you're all right, granfer will take 'ee over to Hayle in the *Twopennard*. They shall never have you!"

————

H.

THE MILPREVE OR ADDER-STONE.

Faith in the properties and origin of the milpreve is, as Mr. Jenner reminds us, the last link between modern Cornwall and the Druids. By them it was held that a bead worn by them as a badge of office, and called *ovum anguinum*, "snake's egg," was formed by a mass of young snakes enclosed within a shell and blown bubble-like into the air, and Pliny in his account of the Druids describes one that he had seen. In Cornwall it was said that multitudes of adders gathered together to produce this bead by hissing on a hazel wand stuck in the ground or by merely joining their froth in one bubble. It was called in Cornish *myl pref*, "a thousand snakes," and held to be an unfailing remedy against snake-bite. In his *Survey of Cornwall*, printed in 1602, Carew describes one in his own possession, and Lhuyd in a letter to Rowland, 1701, mentions the "melprev" as still known in West Cornwall. Borlase quotes all these, but adds no later instance of his own, and it is to William Bottrell that we owe the best account since Lhuyd's of the milpreve. He was the (as usual nameless) "friend" who supplied the excellent milpreve story given by Hunt, and repeated in much the same form in a long footnote in Bottrell's own first series of tales, p p. 148, 149. Bartinney, Velland-uchar, and Trevethow moors are all given by him as sites of adder gatherings and resulting milpreves, produced, according to local belief, by a mass of snakes. More recently the Rev S Rundle met with a "mil-proo" and the old belief still flourishing at Godolphin (*Journal. R. Inst. Cor.*, XI, p.p.

A Ringworm Cure

About eighty years ago there lived at Saint Mellion, near Callington, a dear old dame, by name Ann —, who was noted far and wide for her curative powers. According to those who remember her, she made a celebrated ointment, consisting of chopped pennyroyal and lard, with which she could cure ringworm. Only three applications were needed to effect a perfect cure. On her death, I find she passed on her secrets, as she called them, to her son, who later sold them to various persons in East Cornwall, including a well-known veterinary surgeon.

In writing of ringworm, I am reminded of a so-called "Pellar," at present residing at Callington. In a recent conversation he informed me, that he could cure and transfer ringworm, both in humans and cattle, but he refused to give me any particulars of his methods, except to say that he had cured scores of sufferers in the district, who it appears had to visit him three times on three successive evenings for an effective cure.

Although he is not a Pellar by birth, he claims to have been instructed in the "magic arts" by a witch, in return for a bag of potatoes.

W. H. Paynter

MODERN SURVIVALS OF OLD BELIEFS
By L. J. DICKINSON

THOSE who have lived in Cornwall for many years, and who are in touch with its country-folk, often come across old practices of witchcraft that they formerly thought of as exploded superstions—for instance, about two years ago, a tale was related to me by a woman who worked in my house, about a curious happening in the Holsworthy district. She knew one of the persons herself, and she also averred that the truth of the tale was vouched for by a respectable tradesman in the district. It concerns a farmer and a postman near Holsworthy. The postman delivered letters at the farm, and to save time he made a short cut across some fields where there was no path, and no right-of-way. The farmer forbade his doing so, and they had a great quarrel. Shortly afterwards everything at the farm went wrong ; the crops failed, the pigs died, and the butter wouldn't come. On considering the matter the farmer came to the conclusion that he had been "overlooked," and he went to a white witch to see if his suspicions were true. The witch gave him a glass of water, and told him to gaze into it intently. He did so, and he saw forming on the surface of the water, a face, which was the face of the postman ! He felt so annoyed and angry that he thrust his finger into the eye of the face he saw in the water, and then he came away. Soon afterwards it was observed that the postman had become blind in one eye. It had gradually withered away, apparently for no reason at all, but every one knew it was because the farmer had poked out the eye he saw in the vision in the glass of water!

Besides "ill wishing" or "over-looking," there are charms for benevolent purposes, such as curing ailments, snake bites, rheumatism, removing warts, etc. Here is a remedy for curing a stye in the eye, or what is locally known as a "quillaway." You stroke the eyelid with a Tom-cat's tail three times, three mornings running; and it must be done very early, before the dew is off the ground. Another informant who knew of this practice said a single hair was equally efficacious, but it must be from a cat. In another cure for the same trouble, the charmer stands with a rolling-

---

1 [In Jezegou's *E Korn an Oaled* is a Breton tale in which the putting out of a thief's eye by piercing its reflection in a bucket with a poker is threatened by a *sorser* (wise-man). Evidently another form of the same superstition.—Ed.]

pin and points it at the sufferer, who must say, "What are you pointing at?" The charmer replies, "Not you, not you." The patient then says, "What *are* you pointing at?" "At your eye," answers the charmer; "I drive the stye away," and away it goes! Cats seem to be in favour for medical treatment, even for curing measles. It is recommended by one white witch in my neighbourhood that you should cut off the cat's left ear, and drop three drops of its blood into a wineglass full of spring water. You then administer the remedy to the child who has measles.

Other curious things are recommended in this district. For whooping-cough you fill a little muslin bag full of spiders, tie it round the neck of the patient, who wears it day and night, and the cough departs; for asthma, spiders are again made use of. In this case the webs of spiders must be collected, rolled up into a ltttle ball in the palm of the hand, and then swallowed.

I wonder whether there is a vestige of ancient knowledge behind some of these ancient remedies? Is it possible that there may be an antidote or antiseptic in spiders which forgotten lore was acquanted with, and that practice has continued without the knowledge? We know that ants and bees secrete formic acid from which formaldehyde, and also that common remedy for sore throats, formamint, are made. And I wonder whether there is any electricity in a cat's tail which may stimulate a stye to depart? We know that cats are very electric animals.

There was, till some years ago, an old man in Tintagel, who was always considered to be a "wise-man" or white witch. Old Martin, as he was called, and whom I knew well, had many charms for various troubles, such as warts, sprains, burns, etc. He cured a girl I know, of warts, by what resembles the "absent treatment" given by Christian scientists. The mother of the child went to him for help, and all he asked of her was the *name* of the afflicted one. Then he said, "Go home, her'll be all right," and in a week all the warts had gone. This old man would never take money for his charms—all he would accept was a little tobacco on another day, and the recipients of his benefits were not even allowed to thank him. He had a curious spell for curing sprains. It does not seem quite complete, so perhaps he witheld part of it. What was told to me is this: the charmer must take hold of the injured limb, and say, "As our Saviour went over God's bridge, he caught his toe in a stone and he got a sprain. Then comes Peter who stretched it out, bone to bone, sinew to sinew, skin to skin.

I hope every drop of blood in thy body will run, in the name of the Father, the Son, and Holy Ghost." This was written as Old Martin said it. Another charm of the old man's is for curing boils. He divulged, it when very ill, to the District Nurse, and she confided it to me. The spell has to be recited over the patient, using his or her own name in the right place :—" *Susie Brown*, three angels came from the west. One had fire, the others had water and frost. Out Fire ! In, Water and Frost ! In the name of the Father, the Son and the Holy Ghost."

An old man, in a parish not far from Tintagel, confided to the Rector's wife a way of frustrating the evil intentions of the person who had ill-wished you. This lady is a friend of mine and she handed on the information to me. When you are ill-wished and you know who has done it, you must procure a photograph of that person, and then you write his or her name across the face in the picture, and throw the photograph in the fire. You can't be hurt after that, for it breaks the spell. The old man who told this charm to my friend had been ruined by a law-suit brought against him by an enemy. He longed to obtain a photograph of the ill-wisher, but so far had not been successful.

This tale seems to be a modern version of the ancient method of making a wax image of one's enemy, and then melting it before a fire. Psalm 68, verse 2, probably refers to the same practice : " As wax melteth before the fire, so let the wicked perish at the presence of God." An adaptation of this psalm is used as a charm for curing snake-bite. A former vicar of Bolventor (that lonely parish on the Bodmin Moor), gave me an account of how a dog had been bitten by an adder, and its head had swollen to the size of a football, The charm was repeated over it by a " wise-man " in the locality, and immediately the swelling diminished and the dog recovered. The words used were :—" Let God arise and let His enemies be scattered. Let them that hate Him flee before Him. Like as the smoke vanisheth so shalt thou drive them away, and like as wax melteth at the fire, so let *this poison* perish at the presence of God, in the name of the Father, the Son, and the Holy Ghost. Amen." My informant said that in the case of a human being, *belief* in the efficacy of the charm was necessary, but it did not matter for an animal. He also added that the practice of charming was much resorted to by his parishioners on the moor, and that when their animals are bitten by adders, it is the wise-man who is sent for rather than the veterinary surgeon. Sometimes they sent twelve miles for a charmer of

special ability. He justly said that if the wise-man had not been successful, and the people had suffered loss through the creatures dying in spite of being charmed, the witch would soon have been forsaken for the vet.

It is the success of the wise-man that makes him still so popular, and which is to us such a curious problem.

An Old Charm from Lawhitton

WHEN Edward Lhuyd made his journey into Cornwall in 1700 he kept a note-book which is still preserved at the Bodleian Library, Oxford. In it he recorded the following version of a well-known charm :

"For ye stinging of a long creple, i.e., snake, or any venemous worm :—

Bragg, bragg under ye halse he lay (a halsen stick, i.e., a hazzle), where he lay, he lay full nine fold, from nine fold to eight fold, from eight fold to seven fold, from seven fold to six fold, from six fold to five fold, from five fold to four fold, from four fold to three fold, from three fold to two fold, from two fold to one fold, from one fold to never a fold, out with ye spear & away with ye pain. In ye name of ye Father ye Son & ye Holy Ghost. Amen.

You must strike your hand upon yᵘ place, saying ye same words three times. Probatum est per Agnetam ffrost, out of an old acct. book of one Mr. — Cole, now in ye hands of Mr. Shute of Lawhitton."

His note that Agnes Frost had verified this suggests that he copied it out with the intention of using it, rather than as a curiosity. In the same book he has copied a Latin charm against falling sickness, which consists only of carrying the names of the Three Kings and their gifts, of myrrh, frankincense and gold, on ones person.   R.M.N.

The Thirty Pence Charm

SOME time since I had a conversation with an interesting and intelligent octogenarian, a Mr. Rowe, who has since died. He was a lifelong resident of this parish of St. Neot, a farmer, who resided at a place called Linkindale. The old gentleman told me among other things of a curious observance in which he took part as a youth.

A young woman who was subject to fits arranged through the agency of a young man friend, that thirty young men should attend church on a certain Sunday morning, and each young man brought a penny which was handed to the girls' agent, who thereupon gave the girl half-a-crown in silver in lieu of the coppers. This ritual was a sovereign specific for fits, and in this case it proved efficacious for a long period ; all through her married life, in fact, till she reached an age of over seventy, when the fits returned. I remember the person as an old woman, and have no doubt as to the accuracy of the story. Hunt gives a similar charm for palsy, in which the thirty pence were given by the congregation to the woman herself, one Margery Penwarne of St. —— ; to complete the charm she walked three times around the communion-table, moved out from the wall by the clerk for that purpose, the silver coin being finally made into a ring worn by the patient.

W. Arthur Pascoe.

THE SACRED HARE

About a year ago the Museum Of Witchcraft in Boscastle, North Cornwall, acquired a ceramic statue of a hare. It was supposed to have been unearthed on a caravan site in West Cornwall. The figure is about 4ft 6in in height and carries ritualistic decorations. It may possibly have had a pagan significance.

The belief in hares as magical creatures goes way back in the West Country. It was linked to the Saxon goddess Eostre whose festival was celebrated at Easter time (hence the name). Superstitions abound in Cornwall regarding the hare. If a pregnant woman met a hare, it was once thought, it would give the child a hare lip unless a friend cut off some of the mother's clothing. Because the hare was thought to be a melancholy creature, if you ate its flesh you too would become melancholy. People also thought that the hare changed sex on a yearly basis.

There are also many stories in the West Country about hunters shooting the hare only to discover that they had killed ancient witches, who, once dead, resumed their human form again. A Cornish tale tells of Sir Rose Price who shot at a hare which ran into a cottage at Kerrow. When he and his friends entered the cottage they found an old woman with wounds to her head and hands. Superstitions about hares continued right up until recent times in Cornwall. In 1890, for example, there is a case of a hare being offered as a sacrifice. During building work on an old house in Falmouth the builders refused to carry on with their work until a sacrifice was made to the "outside gods" of a virgin hare, trapped by a virgin boy. Some years later, when repairs were carried out on the roof of the house, the remains of a rabbit were found in a beautifully made coffin near the top of a wall.

Another story concerns a family who were on holiday in North Cornwall in 1934. They had been staying in a hotel near Boscastle and decide they would go for a drive, and then a walk on the moors. Suddenly they came across a large hare sitting on its haunches and screaming at them in a most uncanny fashion. One of the family picked up the creature and calmed it so that eventually the hare hopped quietly away. Back at the hotel they met the landlord and told their story. The man turned pale and told them he could not offer them B&B any longer. They paid their bill and left. Later they were informed by someone in Tintagel that no one but a witch could handle a hare as they had done.

The fear of the hare as totem animal was widespread among fishermen in Cornwall. Until comparatively recently, if a fisherman on his way to boats chanced to meet a woman, a parson or a hare, he turned back, , being convinced that he would have no luck that day. A fairly recent account to do with hares was related to the author by a woman living in Porthleven. She recalls that in her grandfather's time there were two rival families of fishermen. One family had watched the other bring in a huge harvest of pilchards and wished to be revenged upon them. At night, they shot a hare and under cover of darkness pinned the animal's carcass to the mast of the boat. The following morning they watched from their own boat as the fishermen went on boards, then rapidly left in horror. No fishing could be done that day, nor the next, nor the day after that. Eventually the hare was removed from the mast and a ritual purification carried out to remove the "curse." Hares were also feared by miners in Cornwall, and there are many tales of Cornish miners who would not go down a mine and had to turn back to their homes because they had seen the creature gambol across an open field.

There are also legends of ghost hares in the county. At Looe, for example, a white hare is often spotted running to the Jolly Sailor Inn from the direction of Talland. This is thought to be the ghost of a girl who committed suicide and it is also thought to be a warning of imminent danger. Before the use of auxiliary engines, the fishermen of Looe stayed at home if a hare was seen, rather than tempt fate by putting to sea. A white hare was also said to haunt the churchyard at Egloshayle, together with the headless ghost of its hunter who, inclined to disbelieve its supernatural existence, tried to shoot it.

All in all, then, the hare was regarded as a taboo object among the Cornish folk. Since it was quite recognisably an aspect of more than one powerful goddess, it was venerated. To eat the hare was to commit an act of cannabilism. Its body was sacred and its actions were seen as a source of divination. The witch or wise woman could and did change into a hare at will and, under the protection of the ancient Goddess who ruled this creature, she could remain hidden unless killed by a silver bullet. It should be remembered that belief in the sacredness of hares goes back to time beyond recall. Among Hindus, for example, the hare was sacred to the moon because the outline of a hare was discernible at the full disc. The hare was also linked to Freyja, a goddess who enjoyed a considerable following.

Perhaps the most memorable magical charm about the hare is contained in this English folk song:

I shall go into a hare
With sorrow and such and muckle care,
And I shall go in the Devil's name
Ay, till I come home again.

In the Cornish folk tales recorded by Bottrell and Hunt, this was most certainly the general belief.